MASTERING THOUGHT:
(BEFORE IT MASTERS YOU!)

BY MARK WALLER, PH.D. LMFT

WingSpan Press

Printed in the United States of America

Parts of this book are a work of fiction. Names, characters,
settings and incidents are either the product of the author's
imagination or used fictitiously. Any resemblance to actual
events, settings or persons, living or dead, is entirely coincidental.

Published by WingSpan Press, Livermore, CA
www.wingspanpress.com
The WingSpan name, logo and colophon are the trademarks of
WingSpan Publishing.

First Edition 2010
ISBN 978-1-59594-419-1
Library of Congress Control Number: 2010935036

Epigraph

"... all silent thinking is nothing but 'egocentric' speech."
— Lev Vygotsky – the father of Russian Psychology

For a free downloadable audio companion to this book, go to:
www.masteringthought.info

For more information go to:
www.masteringthought.com

DEDICATION:

This book is dedicated to the future of my grandchildren.
I hope they may someday read this and put the ideas in this book
into practice in their lives.
To my grandchildren:
Owen, Liam, and Eleanor.

Contents

TABLE OF FIGURES

ACKNOWLEDGEMENTS:

I would like to thank Dr. Ann Margaret McKillop whose extensive editing of the manuscript was invaluable. I would also like to thank Sarah Doyle and Sharon Newton for the feedback they provided. Here is a big thank you to Karin Wilson of *Wild Woman Design* who designed the cover of this book and the overall look for Mastering Thought. Also, this would not be complete without a mention of my marketing mentor Michele Pariza Wacek. Her suggestions were most valuable.

This book would not have been possible without day to day interaction with hundreds of people who put their faith in the process of Witness Thought Transformation™. I learned so much from all who participated in the teleclasses, as clients in my office, and those who attended my workshops. Without these people my progress would have stopped years ago.

I would like to thank Kancho Cameron Shayne, the founder of Budokon, for his support and belief in my work.

Finally, I would like to thank my wife Sheila for her steady backing of my work and her undying emotional support.

Preface:

The core of this book is two fundamental practices. The first is the revolutionary practice of Witness Thought Transformation™. The best use of this book is to first learn Witness Thought Transformation™ and then put it into in your life in exactly the manner outlined here. All the details you need to learn the practice are listed explicitly in the book. Along with that is an exclusive audio download that is available to you, the reader, at www.masteringthought.info. The download is made available to insure your learning and personal transformation is complete.

Today too many think that the *awakening* is the end of the path. It is not. As human beings we are saddled with emotionally reactive patterns that will continue to burden us even after our *awakening*. Mastery is the path to ultimate freedom. The second practice outlined here is a method of discovering one's *reactive phrases* that trigger defensive/reactive patterns. This leads to Mastery. One of my favorite awakened teachers is Byron Katie who says, "Realization has no value until it is lived." Mastery will release you from the ego's bonds to truly live in freedom.

To help with your personal growth and movement toward Mastery there are many resources and downloads available at www.masteringthought.com. In particular, those seeking Mastery in a relationship will benefit from the Lion/Unicorn material available at the site.

INTRODUCTION:

When I wrote my previous book, *Awakening: Exposing the Voice of the Mosaic Mind*, I never realized how many people could relate to the information about the voice in their head. It seems that very little if anything has ever been written about it, and what was written certainly was not widely circulated. *Awakening* caused such a stir and was such a revolution to so many that it seemed that a book that was more confined and to the point about the voice in the head was in order.

It wasn't so much that the previous book was cumbersome. It was not. But it included many other concepts that were linked to the concept of *Awakening;* the scope of the book swept from relationships to enlightenment. I felt very strongly that bringing these concepts together with information about the influence of the ego-mind would paint a complete picture of the misery of the human condition and how to transform one's life.

That combination turned out to be very helpful, especially to those readers who had been on the path of personal and spiritual growth for many years. *Awakening* provided both the framework and the missing piece of what so many had been looking for for so long.

As a working therapist, I continued to explain the concept of "the voice in your head" and the principles around it to my clients one by one as they came into my office. There is a certain perspective one gets after a book is written and you talk about it and find new and different ways to explain things. Thinking matures, ideas get clarified, and concepts take on a new depth with the collective, lived experience.

This evolving process led me to the conclusion that a simple, straightforward book, limited exclusively to the topic of "the voice in the head," was in order. The ideas around this voice, what it really is, and what to do about it, were very big topics indeed. And since I had spent so much of my clinical and workshop time talking about it and further enhancing my explanation of it, the topic itself seemed to take on a life of its own. Finally, I realized the topic was clearly large enough to warrant an entire book.

This all took place during a time when I was trying to figure out how to *mainstream* the message about the internal voice. Somehow I had to get my message to a greater number of people than those who found their way into my therapy practice.

Meanwhile, I could see in case after case that mastering the internal voice and the mechanism that drove it set people free from emotional and psychological problems. It lifted them to a new level of consciousness where problems weren't problems any more. It was as if all of my knowledge as a therapist had been imbued in my clients merely through teaching them this simple concept.

To say this was amazing was a bit of an understatement. It was as if people increased their IQ in a matter of weeks, sometimes only days. Their ability to have insight increased exponentially. With little guidance they would instantly see the source of long standing ego patterns and destructive behaviors and, in the "seeing," be released. Many even went into a state of intense bliss right in front of me.

The basis of these awakenings was the thought-watching technique that I devised and taught over and over again. After a period of time, I needed a name for this skill that I was teaching – a brand so to speak. So I coined the phrase "witness thought transformation™" and that became the moniker of my work. It seemed to explain the process; witnessing your thoughts leads to a transformation in consciousness.

Mastering Thought (Before it masters You!) This book does far more than lay out some self-help technique. The information contained in this volume is a revolutionary synthesis of brain research and clinical experience. The perspective is totally new and has never been considered before in the context in which it is presented here. To say that "you are not your thoughts" is sort of a new age philosophy and like so much other self-help jargon gets stuck in our heads but has no activation in our lives.

Mastering Thought is a dynamic "knowing" that is like a light going on. Suddenly it is not longer dark and you know it to the core of your being. What is presented here is new Truth that is life-changing. This process works, and you will feel different as a result – a transformation in awareness that cannot be denied.

As a therapist, I am challenged not just to make people feel better but to help them see the world through a whole new set of lenses. Witness Thought Transformation™ does that and more.

Chapter 1: A Mind is a Terrible Thing to Face

This is Duncan's first time in my office. Since it is the first time, he will want to tell me what the problem is. So he does.

"Doc, my head feels like it is going to explode. I can't sleep at night. No matter what I do I can't stop worrying. I am starting to have the shakes and sweats. I can't get out of my head. It won't shut up!"

"Is this a recent phenomenon?"

"Yeah, but my head has always been really noisy. I lie in bed at night and it goes on and on. I would just like to get some relief from it."

I nod knowingly. I have heard this so often. "You just can't turn it off, can you?"

"Nope. And I'll tell you something else. I am drinking and smoking pot every night just to get myself to calm down. Even at that, I still can't get my thoughts to stop swirling around. I mean, the stuff does help me calm down, and eventually I do fall asleep. Before I was doing that, I was sleeping a couple hours, then I would wake up and obsess about one thing or another and then fall back to sleep. This happened several times a night."

I look at him and I can tell by his expression that he is sincerely distressed. "I'll bet this obsessive thinking happens off and on all day long as well," I speculate.

He nods and says, "The only relief I seem to get from it is when I am interested in something or working on a project – you know, concentrating."

"That makes sense. That is a key to understanding the process and how the brain works around this thing we call the voices in the head."

Duncan looks up at me. It is as if I interrupted his internal process and he is now completely present with me in the room for the first time. "What do you mean 'how the brain works'?"

"Well, what you have just described offers some real insight into how this all plays out in the brain. You said that when you are focusing or concentrating, the internal dialog seems to stop. Is that right?"

"Right."

"So it appears that self-talk and concentration are mutually exclusive, meaning that you cannot do both at the same time."

Duncan gets a quizzical look on his face. "Yeah?"

"In other words, your experience is that you cannot talk to yourself and pay attention to something you're interested in at the same time. Let me give you an example. Let's say you are watching your favorite TV program. If you are really involved in the plot, action, whatever, you are not at the same time in your head commenting, 'I'm really involved in this program.'"

"Oh, I see what you mean. It's like I can't walk and chew gum at the same time."

I chuckle, "I suppose it is a lot like that."

"I am a worrier. I notice that I spend a lot of time worrying about money, my job, whether or not there is a crack in the road, if I remembered to turn off the stove when I left the house."

"I'll bet all of that worrying doesn't seem to change the outcome of anything or make things better, does it?"

"No it doesn't, Doc. It just makes me feel tense, ill at ease. Sometimes I will just start sweating for no apparent reason and there is a sick feeling in the pit of my stomach. I know you are going to tell me that I am crazy. I just don't want my wife to find out I am crazy."

I laugh. "Duncan, don't worry. She is just as crazy as you are," I chuckle. "We're all crazy as long as we are dominated by the noise in our heads."

"We are?"

"Of course, Duncan. Understand that you are not the only one that has this problem. Each and every one of us is dominated by one or more internal dialogues at any given point. It is the bane of humanity."

On Duncan's face I can see an expression of both surprise and relief. "I'm not the only one whose head won't shut up?"

"There is a lot of silent suffering out there. Just because someone looks calm and 'normal' doesn't mean they aren't paddling like hell on the inside."

"I guess that makes sense. Philosophically I know you're right, but when I am compulsively regurgitating every possible negative scenario in my mind, it is hard to have the awareness that the guy next to me is doing it too."

"Yes, and what is interesting is that there are common themes to all of this. Granted, you might be talking to yourself about your blond wife and the next guy is obsessing over his brunette wife, but the story is similar. There isn't a lot of the internal landscape that differs from one person to another."

Duncan nods and I continue, "What I have found talking to hundreds of people who walk through my door is that the story lines are very much the same from one person to the other. It is as if humanity hasn't had an original thought in thousands of years."

He laughs and says, "I am sure my thoughts are not particularly original either. There is sort of a sickening repetition to it all. The question is, 'how do I get rid of it?'"

"Better than getting rid of it, how about making it irrelevant?"

"What do you mean, Doc?"

"What I mean is that suppose we can't get rid of it. Suppose we just pay no more attention to it?"

Duncan looks at me like I am crazy. "How can I do that? It's me. I have to pay attention to it. I don't have a choice!"

"Or so it would seem," I chuckle.

#

Pat and Angie, my former clients, have referred their friends to me for marriage counseling. I am excited to meet them and get to work on behalf of their Awakening. I am sure that both Pat and Angie have already analyzed their friends and filled their heads with hope for a better marriage and a better life. Of course I am just assuming this since it so powerfully happened for them.

Ed and Marissa walk into my office and we exchange pleasantries.

When the initial energy dies down, Ed pipes up, "I'm the Lion and she's the Unicorn. So there. I just saved us all a months of therapy." Ed leans back in the chair and lets out a satisfied guffaw.

Marissa rolls her eyes and punches Ed in the arm. "Sheezuz, will you let the doctor do his job?" She turns to me and explains, "I'm sorry, doctor, ever since Pat and Angie told us your Lion/Unicorn theory, Ed has been ranting and raving."

"I read his book," Ed shouts. "It's awesome. It explains why I've been such an ass all these years. You will have to admit I am trying now that I can understand that I've been scaring hell out of you for nine years."

"Yes, Ed, I can tell you are trying. The house has been much more peaceful lately."

I smile ruefully to myself. The use of the word 'peaceful' punctuates their system of pursuit and avoidance. "So, obviously you two have started to see a good deal about the relationship dynamics that are going on between you. Why come to me?"

"Well, after seeing the huge change in both Angie and Pat, we wanted to make sure we weren't missing anything for ourselves," Marissa states.

Ed chimes in, "Yes, if we can have a better relationship, I am willing to do anything. I am only now beginning to realize that there are emotions and reactions inside of me that I have never noticed before. I am wondering if there might be more I am not seeing."

"I have to agree with Ed. We really want to get the most out of life – out of our life together. I am willing to do my part too," says Marissa.

I can feel a satisfying glow fill the room as I look at these two very earnest people who want a better life. "You know, you two have made my day."

"How?" asks Ed.

"You just took *responsibility*. You know, my office is full of people who won't take personal responsibility. They want to blame their partner. They tell me that their lives would be better if only the other person would change. They never once stop and ask if maybe they might be part of the problem.

"When people come in and are willing to look at themselves and simply do the work of personal change for its own sake, it makes me feel like I am not wasting my time. So thanks for presenting yourselves like adults instead of children."

Marissa says, "I am absolutely willing to look at myself. I know that Ed tends to be the more verbal of the two of us, but I know that I am up to something inside too. We have had years of conflict, and for a long time I thought it was all him. Then one day I saw how I was withholding and judging and punishing. In my own way, I was just as angry as he was. I knew I needed to address what was going on inside of me. It wasn't just Ed. That's why I am here. I know I have a part in all of this. I also know I don't always see what I am doing. I feel like I need new eyes."

"Wow, Marissa, you have absolutely come to the right place, because what I am going to teach you is a practice that will absolutely give you a new set of eyes!"

"I hope that goes for me too," says Ed. "I need new eyes. The one thing I have realized about myself is that I am domineering, arrogant, and pompous. It wasn't pleasant to see this about myself. But now I want to tear the thing out by the roots. Do major surgery on me, Doc. I am sick of Ed. I will do whatever it takes."

I look at these two people and take in their sincerity. It feels like a warm bath that is comforting and relaxing. Outside I can hear birds and the sound of the occasional car as it careens down the street. I notice that outside it is starting to get dark.

"You know, Einstein said, 'No problem can be solved from the same consciousness that created it. We must look at the world anew.' So that is what we are going to do here. I am going to teach you how to look at the world anew. So there is your new set of eyes."

Ed pipes up, "I'm ready, Doc."

I say, "Oh, and one more thing, you will not be rolling on the floor coughing up pea soup and reliving every bad thing that ever happened to you."

"I was hoping you would say something like that. I dread dredging up the past. But I thought that's what therapy was all about," says Marissa.

"What I am going to show you is that your brain is dredging up the past and hijacking you with it in real time, almost on a moment-by-moment basis. This hijacking is so complete and yet so subtle that it has been going unnoticed for years. It is subtle, not because it is small. This thing that goes on in our heads is *huge*. It is subtle because it has repeated itself *so often* for so many years *we don't even know it's there anymore*."

"Gotcha, Doc, but how are we being hijacked? I mean, in exactly what way?" asks Ed.

"You have a hijacker living in your head." I say flatly.

"I do?"

"Yes, it is called thought, or more precisely *verbal* thought."

Ed looks confused.

"You know the voice in your head, the voice that sounds like you talking to you? That is the source of the hijacking."

"Oh," says Ed, "I get it. Stinkin' thinkin'. I thought this might have something to do with positive thinking."

"Actually, it is deeper than that. The problem turns out to be *thought* itself. And that is where all the trouble is coming from. Thought is the source of all human misery."

"I'm sure you're right, Doc. But I am positive it is the source of all of my misery!"

Marissa has been listening intently and asks, "I have a question. How is this supposed to help our relationship?"

"That's a great question. The cycle in your relationship is related to thought. Thought is the source of meaning and meaning is the trigger for emotional reactivity. It is the reactivity that keeps the cycle going in your relationship."

"You mean when I avoid?"

"Yes, Marissa, a defense that you are all too familiar with is avoidance. I see you really have been talking with Pat and Angie about the pattern in your relationship."

Marissa looks at Ed and rolls her eyes. "Oh yes, they nailed my *m.o.* right away. It was so obvious that I couldn't *avoid* it." Everyone laughs at her play on words.

"Right, you react by avoiding when *thought* tells you there is going to be *conflict*."

Ed chimes in, "Then I see that as rejection and take it personally and that makes me angry. So it becomes a self-fulfilling prophecy."

I smile and say, "Yes, but it is all driven by thought . Marissa's thought is about conflict and your thought is about rejection and you're off to the races. The tragedy is that the thoughts, which are driving perception and meaning in this example, are not true. There needn't be conflict and there is no rejection."

Ed chuckles to himself and says, "It is a little like I am holding a gun to her head and screaming, 'why are you rejecting me?'"

"And I am shrinking in terror from someone who just wants to be loved."

"Right, so intellectually you see exactly what is happening between you two. Now it is up to me to give you a powerful tool so you can begin to see this at the gut level in real time, as it's actually happening."

"You mean we won't be using willpower to overcome these tendencies? I mean to get out of the cycle?" asks Ed.

"You will find that willpower won't be needed. What you need is a new set of eyes, or rather new perception. Your perception is where the hijacking is taking place. Most people look to their behavior. They come in and say to me, 'I need to be less angry.' But anger is a behavior that is a symptom of a misinterpretation of events taking place around a person. It all starts with perception, that is, the way we make meaning. If our meaning making is predetermined, we will react in a certain way no matter the facts or the situation. So rather than work on better behavior, we need to find a way of accessing a less distorted perception."

Marissa looks at me and smiles, "How long is this miracle going to take? It sounds like we are undoing a life time of learning here."

"We are and it will take about three weeks," I answer. "Think of it this way. What if your house was being robbed every night and you went to the wisest person on earth to find out how to prevent it from happening in the future. What would that wise man tell you to do?"

"Shoot him with a gun!" exclaims Ed.

"Arrest him?" asks Marissa.

I chuckle. "Remember, the thief is coming in the night. So before you can shoot him or arrest him what do you need to do?"

"Catch him," Ed says in frustration.

"No, Ed, think. It's night."

"Oh! Find him. I have to find him to shoot him."

"How are you going to find him?"

Marissa has a sudden realization. "I know, I know."

"What, Marissa?"

"To find the thief you have to turn on the light!" She smiled with a look of confidence.

"Perfect deduction. That's what we are going to do here. We are going inside your head, and we are going to turn on the light."

CHAPTER 2: WHAT IS THOUGHT?

No discussion of thought would be complete without some reference to the brain. For the discussions in this book it is useful to think of a hierarchy with a twist. We each have three brains, each one on top of the other. In the uterus of a pregnant woman, this is especially easy to spot and has been documented in video studies as each brain represents a separate developmental stage as the fetus grows. The first brain has been labeled the reptilian brain since it mimics, in many respects, the functions of the brain in reptiles. It keeps us breathing and warm. It keeps us alive biologically.

The next brain is a set of primitive structures called the Limbic System. The Limbic System is sometimes called the Midbrain or the Mammalian Brain. It is all about emotions and survival, those functions that we tend to share with other mammals like dogs and cats and primates. Much of this book will be devoted to probing the mysteries of the Limbic System.

Last, but not least, is the Cerebral Cortex. We tend to think of the Cerebral Cortex as the adult brain, or at least that which functions to distinguish us from our animal friends. The main function that distinguishes humans is that we have language, which is an ability that is unique to the Cerebral Cortex.

But wait! Language, as it turns out, is processed and expressed as a function of the left side of the brain. The entire right hemisphere is nonverbal. Not only is the right hemisphere nonverbal, but the Limbic System and the reptilian brain are also nonverbal. So language is the sole purview of the left side of the brain.

Much has been written about the difference between the left hemisphere and the right hemisphere. The left brain thinks logically, the right thinks holistically and so it goes. But for our purposes here, in answering the question what is thought, this hemispheric division neatly divides categories of thinking into verbal thought and nonverbal thought.

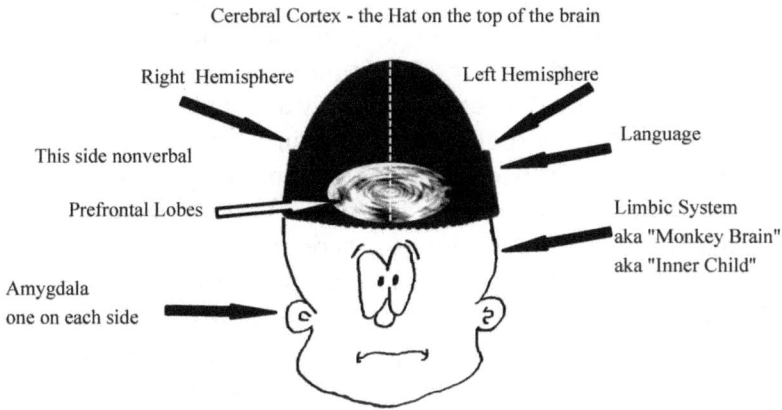

Cerebral Cortex - the Hat on the top of the brain

Right Hemisphere   Left Hemisphere

This side nonverbal   Language

Prefrontal Lobes

Limbic System
aka "Monkey Brain"
aka "Inner Child"

Amygdala
one on each side

Figure 1: Stylized view of the brain

NON VERBAL THOUGHT

Nonverbal thought can be categorized as thinking in pictures, thinking in music, thinking in mathematics. Other forms of nonverbal thought involve spatial orientation or the ability to manipulate shapes with our imagination. You might notice that is it hard to talk about nonverbal thought since it does not lend itself to verbalization.

The Mind's Eye is nonverbal. Nonverbal thought is mechanical, involves modeling, and manipulating. Of course we have all heard of body language – that's nonverbal. The nonverbal is a level of communication that seems so mysterious to us. And yet the first interaction we have with our mothers from the day we are born is all nonverbal. In fact, the first year or more of human development is nonverbal. A baby's entire developmental task in the first year is to learn how to read the mother's central nervous system by studying her face. This is done with the right orbital frontal cortex which is nonverbal. A two year old has 20 times more neural connections than an adult, nearly all from nonverbal learning.

The entire natural world is an expression of nonverbal thought. The nonverbal is visual, kinesthetic, and synesthetic. It is meant to be touched, felt, and lived. Nonverbal thought is experienced now – it is the experience of *now*.

It is common to relegate nonverbal thought to thinking in pictures.

So let's expand our discussion and change the phrasing slightly. Let's talk about nonverbal intelligence.

I have a cat named Ronnie. When he was fairly young, he learned to open that back screen door by hooking his claws into the screen to pull it open. I have pondered this for a long time. How does Ronnie experience this nonverbal learning? There is certainly a *knowing* that came with the learning, but it is nonverbal. By that I mean he doesn't stand in front of the screen and say to himself, "Now I am going to open the screen." There is no verbalization going on since he doesn't know language. (By the way, Ronnie has never learned to close the screen!)

When I ponder what Ronnie's internal experience is, it feels weird. Does he experience this learned behavior in pictures as a knowing? What is his experience? We often hear the phrase "dumb animals." My experience is that they are anything but dumb. He smiles when he is happy. He rubs me when he wants to be close. He even pantomimes certain stances when he wants me to do something for him.

For instance, when his brother is outside and wants to come in, Ronnie will stand on his hind legs and paw at the door frantically. This means Ronnie wants to go out or knows that his brother wants in. The dumb humans he lives with eventually figure out what Ronnie is trying to say and get it right! He will even go and stare at his water bowl when it is empty until we get the message and fill the bowl.

Is this instinct? It is some survival mechanism? No, it is intelligence being expressed nonverbally. Since we live so much of the time in our left hemisphere, the nonverbal world remains a mystery. We minimize it, we discount it.

And yet what is ironic about this is that our interaction with other people is defined by the nonverbal parts of the brain. Those who have right brain deficits, especially up in the front of the brain, have trouble processing the emotions related to social contact. Asperger's Disorder, which is a mild form of autism, is an example of this. Young adults with this disorder have a lot of trouble interacting with people because they simply cannot process the social cues and emotions that we all take for granted. Nonverbal thought is hugely important and a necessary part of living.

We often have the mistaken impression that right-brain thinking is kind of spacey and airy-fairy, when in fact; it is very much down to earth in the here and now. We just have a hard time identifying with it since we pay no attention to it. By the way, I am not referring here to what some people often label as "right brain thinking," that is, creative and artistic thinking.

The right brain is about getting the big picture; it is about integrating parts into the whole. I believe it is possible to have magnificent nonverbal intelligence and not be the least bit artistic. I have had many male clients who were machinists. These guys operate computer driven metal lathe machines that require an enormous amount of holistic thinking. I have found these men to be true geniuses because of their ability to see the whole and program the machine to dig it out of a lump of metal. These specialists are very much underappreciated in our society, but they are the creative equivalent of sculptors.

While verbal thought dominates the left hemisphere of the brain, nonverbal thought is the product of the right hemisphere. Here multiple processors operate in parallel giving the entire sense of each moment. It is as if all of the puzzle pieces come together in each instant and there is an "aha" of awareness of what the experience of life is. We are like a laser light of awareness illuminating the holograph of life as it unfolds so that we can be fully immersed in the experience of it. Dr. Jill Bolte Taylor says in her book, *My Stroke of Insight*:

> To the right mind, no time exists other than the present moment, and each moment is vibrant with sensation. Life or death occurs in the present moment. The experience of joy happens in the present moment. Our perception and experience of connection with something that is greater than ourselves occurs in the present moment. To our right mind, the moment of *now* is timeless and abundant. (2006, p. 30)

She goes on to say that the present moment is a time when everything and everyone are connected together as *one*. The right side does not like lines, borders, rules and regulations. It thinks outside the box. It is a dreamer who likes to ask questions about possibilities and looks for the intuitive flash as opposed to the logical deduction. When we are not worrying and carefree we are in our *right* mind. The right brain is about imagination, similarities, and relationships to the whole. Getting back to how we process emotions, the right prefrontal cortex is the empathetic brain that allows us to understand the emotional experiences of someone else. Compassion is not logical, but rather is *right*.

Nonverbal thought therefore is compassionate, empathetic,

understanding the big picture, living in the present moment, seeing how the world interrelates and feeling at one with all things. It would seem that what we have all been looking for has been hiding in the right side of our heads all of our lives.

This book is about unlocking that and gaining access to it. But surprisingly there is nothing we need to do to get from here to there. There is no operation to be done on the right side of the brain to open that door; it has always been open. It turns out that something has been blocking it. Humorously, this blocking has come from a simple misunderstanding. Clearing up this misunderstanding is the subject of this book. The goal is to make the world of nonverbal thought accessible.

Verbal Thought

What is verbal thought? Simple. It is the voice in your head that sounds like *you* talking to *you*. This is the majority of verbal thought. The rest might be the imaginary voice of a parent, a spouse, or other people who live in our heads. The short of it is that verbal thought is the words of your language in your mind.

But before we get into this further, let's take a look at the left hemisphere. By the way, the vast majority of us are left-brain dominant. That goes for left-handers too. Hand dominance is not a predictor of brain dominance.

Some of us are right-brain dominant, which means everything I am saying is inside out or reversed or whatever. How do you know if everything in your head is flipped? You must be tested. Just because you are more creative or artistic doesn't mean you are right--brain dominant. All it means is that those functions normally associated with the left hemisphere are taking place in the right and vice versa.

By comparison to the right hemisphere, the left brain is into sequences, details, facts, and organization. The passage of time is a function of the left side of the brain. The left hemisphere is logical, deductive; it likes to arrange things, categorize things and label things.

When you give a woman a flower, she takes in the entire experience with the right hemisphere. However, she might be tempted to dissect the flower with her left hemisphere into the various parts of the flower naming them in sequence. While we enjoy music with our right hemisphere, we keep the beat with our left.

When we are caught up in analyzing the remembered past or

worrying about an imagined future we are in our left brain. When we are into the story of "me," we are using the left brain. In fact, *drama* is a function of the left hemisphere. Our left hemisphere is where we look for a sense of control, authority, and security. It is where we judge, criticize, compare, predict and anticipate.

As I said, verbal thought is the words of your language in your mind. What does this mean? It means that your internal dialogue, what scientists call the *dialogical self*, is going to speak in the language that you use every day. So if you were born and raised in Mexico, your inner voice is speaking Spanish. If you were born in Italy, your dialogical self is speaking Italian. If you were born in the U.S., well, you get the picture.

Now here is a curious thing that I have discovered talking to people who have moved to the U.S. from other countries. If you were born in a non-English speaking country and move to the U.S., as you assimilate and learn English your internal voice begins to speak English. In fact, people in these circumstances actually begin to dream in their new language! As we will see later, the implications of this are huge.

Verbal thought is often directed. Directed verbal thought might be when I am remembering a script or recalling directions to someone's house. I am directing the verbal rehearsal in my head. The illusion is that it is *we* who are doing the directing. You will find out later that this is rarely the case.

Most verbal thought is the uncontrollable, compulsive, reflexive thought. That is when my inner voice is talking to me about *me*. Most verbal thought is in the form of explanations, regurgitations, and rationalizations. This is either about the remembered past or the imagined future. In other words, we are explaining ourselves to ourselves. Verbal thought is your own self-talk.

If that seems strange, consider this. If we are talking to ourselves about ourselves, at some level we must know what we are thinking about prior to thinking it! What I mean is that, *knowing* must come before thinking. This knowing also includes our motivation for thinking as well as any internal emotional chemistry that is driving thinking. Therefore, the brain must have access to information prior to verbal thought. This points to an important question. Of what value is verbal thought?

What is interesting about verbal thought is that there is always a subjective *me* and some kind of object external to *me*. This "me" is the thinker. Of course the object or audience is also *me*. The important point here is that this recursive, reflexive internal dialogue generates a sensation of subjectivity called *me*. We will see later that our misinterpretation of this is the bane of humanity.

If the inner speaker is *me*, then everything it is speaking about is "not" me. Right? If I am having the subjective experience of being the thinker of verbal thought, then everything that is not the thinker is an object of the thinking. But consider this. What if the *thinker* was an object of something else that is really who we are? That would mean that the thinker is an object and the experience of *me* is nothing more than a sensation or a construct of the experience of verbal thought.

SUBJECTIVITY

I would like to consider the topic of *subjectivity,* if only briefly. In the framework of nonverbal vs. verbal thought, subjectivity becomes a bit of a Gordian knot. So let's define subjectivity. One simple way of defining subjectivity is the mental state we experience when we encounter an object. Some philosophers use the word "Qualia" to describe this. It means what it's *like* to have an experience.

Let's say you and I are both having a migraine. The discomfort is subjective since my experience of pain cannot be known by you and vice versa. If we could describe it, it would become an object. Another example is for me to say to you, "I am experiencing purple." We both know it is impossible for you to know my experience of purple.

Subjectivity is that which observes an object. So we can have objects in the mind as well as in the world. A mental picture of a flower, for instance, is an *object* in the mind's eye. I will concede that some people define everything mental as subjective and, in a sense of the word, it is. But in another sense, subjectivity is the perspective one has that highlights mental objects. Anything observable or making an appearance in our field of awareness can be said to be objective. Therefore, the field of awareness is the ultimate in subjectivity. There is an aspect of an observing *me* that is the ultimate subjectivity, or so it would seem. Is this "me and that which is not me" the ultimate subject object relationship?

Looking at the left hemisphere this all makes at least a little bit of sense. There is a subjective *me* that is experiencing a *migraine* or *purple*. But if we look at this from the point of view of the right hemisphere the question immediately arises, who is this *me*? Is the right mind aware that *me* lives in the left mind? Let's take this a step further. Does the right hemisphere experience subjectivity? If it does this raises a huge question.

Does this *me* that we think we are exist as anything but an object in consciousness. The consciousness of who?

We can further reduce the question to this, is nonverbal thought an object of a thing called *me*? Since the *story of me* is a product of the left hemisphere, the subjective *me* that we all experience must be, in fact, objective and not subjective. Since only half of our brain is experiencing this *me,* there is, by comparison, part of the brain that experiences "no me."

Is it possible that personal experience, anything that has the feeling of *me* associated with it, is an object of some other aspect of existence? I don't think it would be accurate to say that nonverbal thought is subjective. So both verbal and nonverbal thought is objective.

The subjective experience of verbal thought, that of the observer, the one who knows, the internal speaker (what the Buddhists would call the *witness*), are all aspects of left hemispheric verbal thought. In order for thought to be verbal, there has to be a speaker of the thought and a hearer of the thought. Both of those aspects of verbal thought are, as a matter of necessity, artifacts of verbal thought and not some vast subjectivity that is experiencing verbal thought. So there is no inner knower, thinker, observer, doer, person, self, individual. Oh my God Mark, you have lost your mind!

Back to my cat, Ronnie. He never has the experience of *me*. For him, nothing is personal. There is only the experience of what is. Since Ronnie doesn't experience *self,* everything must be categorized as subjective. But wait. That's not right! His nonverbal experience must surely be objective, but objective in reference to what? In his universe there is no *me*. There is only this cat-consciousness, whatever that is, that embraces everything as objective experience. Or the other even weirder possibility is that since there is no *me*, everything is part of the whole. The objective and subjective merge into one. Ronnie looks out at the world and, if he could talk, says, "I am that!"

Please don't misunderstand me. I know I can't prove anything here in a few short paragraphs. What I am trying to do is to indicate that any discussion of verbal vs. nonverbal thought brings up some troublesome issues; one of the issues is that it may be quite accurate to say that there is no subjective aspect of our awareness called "me."

Chapter 3: The Monkey Brain

Duncan and I have traded pleasantries and now it is time to go to work.

"Okay, Doc, how am I going to fix my head?"

"The first thing I am going to do is to give you a bit of a brain anatomy lesson."

"Oh my God, Doc. Please don't get technical on me."

I know Duncan is kidding me. He is a bright, intelligent person who is more than capable of handling a little technical detail. But people do squawk when confronted with anything that looks like it might be mentally demanding. Since, we each have this sophisticated computer in our heads, you would think that more of us would be mildly curious as to how it works.

"Okay, Duncan, let's start by assuming you actually have a brain. Then we will see if you can use it," I chuckle good-naturedly.

Duncan chortles, "I guess I'm going to finally use my brain for more than a hat rack."

I get up and walk to my whiteboard and draw an ellipse. "Okay, here is the brain."

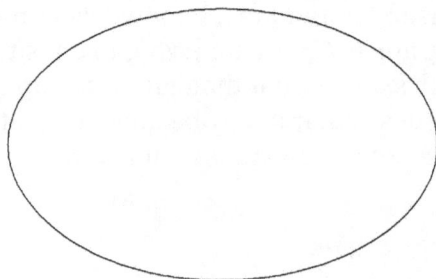

Figure 2: The Brain

Inside the ellipse I draw a figure that is meant to look like the head of a child. "I know what you're going to say, 'don't quit my day job to become an artist."

Duncan shrugs his shoulders, "I'm not a critic."

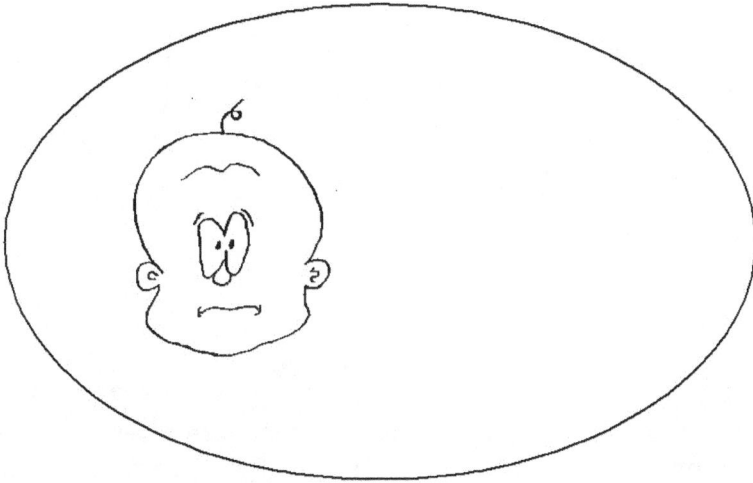

Figure 3: The Limbic System

"Okay, this is supposed to look like a little kid. It represents a part of the brain called the Limbic System. The Limbic System is all about flight or fight, anger or fear, survival. It is the brain's emotional Grand Central Station. And, perhaps most importantly, it is the engine that drives most of your self-talk. I call the Limbic System 'the Monkey Brain.' I call it that because it is the part of the brain that we share with other mammals. You know like dogs, cats, and primates; like monkeys."

"Okay. How come I have never heard of this, what did you call it?"

"The Limbic System."

"How come I've never heard of it before?" Duncan asks.

"I don't know, but I will tell you we are learning more and more about it and its importance.

"The really important thing to know right now is that the Limbic System is completely wired up by the time you are 5 years old or sooner." I stand up and place a caption under the child's head on the board.

"Okay, so . . ." Duncan is looking at me sideways and glancing at the board.

"Just wait a minute, Duncan, there is another part to the point I am making." I walk up to the board and draw a line in the brain.

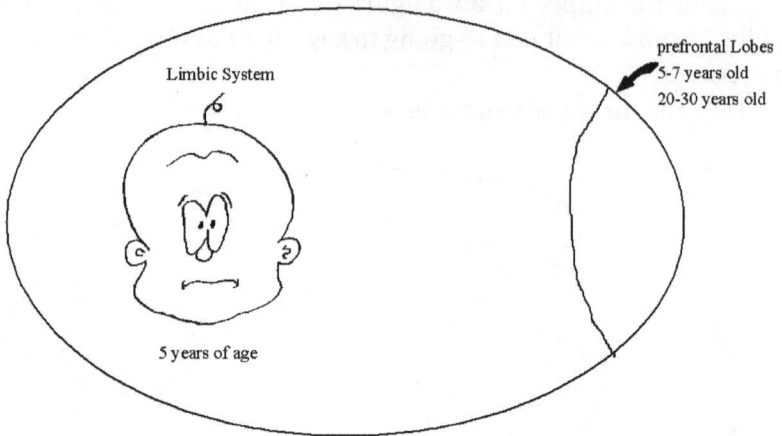

Figure 4: A 15 year gap

"In the front of the brain, in the forehead, are a set of structures called the 'prefrontal lobes.' The purposes of the prefrontal lobes are many. They include focus and concentration, insight, impulse control, and many researchers say, decision making. You will see later that I don't agree entirely with that. But the main job of the prefrontal lobes for our purposes is self-reflection. If I ask you to tell me your thoughts or to guess what someone else is thinking, you would immediately activate the prefrontal area. Whenever we are thinking about thinking or observing our internal *selves*, we use this front area of the brain."

I walk to the board and write numbers down next to the prefrontal lobes. "It turns out that the prefrontal area does not start dramatic development until we are 5 to 7 years of age and they don't stop until we are 20 to 30."

Duncan studies the diagram carefully and says, "Holy cow, does that mean what I think it means?"

"Oh, trust me, it is even worse than anyone has ever dreamed. If we assume that the prefrontal lobes are like the *adult* brain and the Limbic System is the *child* brain, you can see that the child has a 15 year head start in development. When you consider the fact that *thought* is heavily influenced by this, it gets even scarier."

"Yeah, but you called it the monkey brain. What you are really saying is that the monkey is in charge!" Duncan has a look of total shock on his face.

"Yes, by the time we are mature enough to do anything about it, the monkey has been in charge for many years and has tentacles of its patterns of perceiving and behaving entwined deeply throughout the rest of the brain. The adult brain comes along so much later that all it can do is complain that life isn't going the way we want it to."

"Wow. I have a monkey in my head and it's in charge. That explains a lot."

I gesture toward the board and add, "But think of it this way. If the Limbic System is completely wired up by the time we are five years old, then those experiences that we have in the first five years are critical to our development. In other words, the first five years determine what kind of a monkey we have living in our heads. Let me just add that five years of age is somewhat arbitrary. Certain kinds of emotional events that happen when we are six can be vitally important. What happens at twelve has nowhere near the impact on us, by contrast."

Duncan looks at the board and then at me. "But I wasn't abused as a child. I thought I had a relatively decent childhood. Are you saying my parents are to blame?"

"Parents bear a significant responsibility for what happens to children in those first five years, but I am by no means talking about abuse. Imperfect parents have imperfect children. At that age, everything helps wire up the brain. So if your monkey is more of an orangutan and mine is more of a chimpanzee that is a reflection of the stress or lack of it in those formative years. But all of this is beside the point, Duncan. The point is, do you want a monkey, healthy or not, running your life, or controlling your thoughts?"

"Well, no."

"Okay then. Forget about abuse, parents, and all of that. You have a very primitive and powerful part of your brain that is in nearly complete control of your life. And I've got news for you."

"What?"

"The monkey has a voice."

"You mean, in addition to everything else, I have a monkey talking in my head?"

"No, I am saying the *monkey is what's talking*."

"What do you mean? I don't hear a monkey talking in my head."

"I am afraid that you do."

Duncan looks at me incredulous and asks, "What does it sound like?"

I smile and say, "It sounds like *you* talking to *you*."

#

Ed and Marrisa have known about the pattern in their relationship from their discussions with their friends and my former clients, Pat and Angie. They are aware that one partner is more passive and tends to avoid conflict to maintain emotional distance and the other partner is more aggressive and tends to pursue to maintain the emotional connection. So after I discuss the Limbic System with them in much the same fashion I had done with Duncan, Ed has a question.

"Are you going to tell us that the Limbic System has a role in relationships? I mean it makes sense."

"Well, think about when we learn about relationships. We learn about relationships at just the time the Limbic System is in the process of massive development. This is when we have our first relationship."

Marissa looks at me and then at Ed as if to check out if it is safe to talk. "So you are referring to our relationship with our mothers?"

"Actually, no, I am referring here to the first social relationship which may or may not be with our mothers. In other words, from birth through the attachment phase, which ends around 3 years of age, an infant must bond with the mother, assuming there is a mother to bond with. But during that time they have very little sense of being a separate individual. Everything, including mom, is an extension of themselves in their world. Ironically, this is a core truth and not a misperception! But that is another discussion."

Ed smiles, "Doc, you're toying with me."

"Sorry, Ed, I digress. Anyway, around three or four years of age, the child has a separate identity and he or she enters a developmental phase where the task is to interact with another person. Of course because of their age, this interaction is directed mainly by the Limbic System. What this means is that there are a lot of emotions and overtones of survival involved."

"You mean we think we might die?" asks Marissa.

"Actually, a relationship to a four year old is really a life or death matter, in a very real sense. The monkey thinks if it can't get love, security, acceptance or the fulfillment of some emotional need, it might die."

"My God, Doc, that seems a little intense. Does it have to be so serious?" asks Ed.

"I don't know, but whatever happens in that first relationship imprints the Limbic System and sets the trajectory for the rest of relationships throughout the person's life."

I clear my throat and settle back in my chair. "This first relationship is not necessarily with our mothers. It might just as easily be with our fathers. I have no idea how we make this choice. All I know is the impact of this choice and how that relationship turns out impacts us for the rest of our lives. And it drives our thinking around relationships on a moment by moment basis.

"What I want you to understand is that since the Limbic System is in charge of this whole thing, that first relationship has a goal for some kind of emotional fulfillment. In other words, there is some need we have that is fulfilled by being connected to another person. This boils down to one of two basic needs; the need for approval and the need for safety."

Marissa's face lights up. "Oh, I get it, Lions and Unicorns."

"Yes, and it is all tied in with flight or fight, predators and prey, approach and withdrawal. There are a lot of facets of this that describe the dynamic. But more importantly for our discussion is that this dynamic operates as a backdrop that drives our thinking in real-time. "

I search for an example of what I am talking about. "Let's say you are walking up the stairs to go into your house . . ."

"We don't have stairs," Ed pipes up.

Marissa slugs him in the arm.

"As you reach for the door, you know your partner is on the other side of the door. Your brain immediately fires off a series of thoughts that prepare you to go into the house. The Limbic System is the dynamic engine that fuels those thoughts. Now these thoughts are huge, emotion-packed thoughts, but they have been firing off in a variety of circumstances all of our lives and we don't even notice them anymore. But when we walk through that door, we are in a state of readiness for what happens next. All of this happens completely outside of our awareness."

Marissa looks at Ed then turns to me. "Am I the only one that is in the room that doesn't understand what you just said?"

I ask Marissa, "Can we do a little exercise? Would you be willing?"

"Sure," she says. I am a bit surprised at her willingness.

"Okay, I want you to imagine that Ed is on his way home and you hear his car in the driveway. Now you hear him coming up the walkway or whatever, and he opens the door. As I was describing this, what thoughts did you notice?"

"I didn't notice any thoughts."

"So let's try this again. I want you to listen to my voice. As you picture

21

what I am describing, just notice the thoughts and feelings you have inside."

Marissa settles back in her chair as if to concentrate better. "Okay, shoot."

"You know that Ed is on his way home and you hear his car in the driveway. His car door closes and you can hear his footsteps coming up the walk. Finally he turns the doorknob and walks in. As I was describing that, what went through your mind?"

"I couldn't see anything at first and then I noticed that I was wondering what kind of mood he was in."

"Okay, as you noticed that, did you get any kind of feeling in your body?"

Marissa gets a surprised look on her face. "I got nervous. I am still nervous. I can feel it in my stomach now!"

I lean forward in my chair. "Isn't that fascinating? Shake that out of your body."

Marissa shakes her arms and wiggles in the chair, then giggles.

"Now, let me take you back to when you were a little girl. Somebody is coming home. You hear the car door and the footsteps and as the door opens you notice how you are feeling. What do you experience as I take you back in time?"

Marissa looks surprised. "I am feeling nervous again."

I speak softly as I ask, "Take a look now. Who is coming through the door?"

Marissa frowns as she looks inside and says, "It's my mother."

"Why are you nervous?"

"Because she would always yell at me if the house wasn't perfect the way she wanted it to be."

"What do you mean?"

"Well, I was supposed to clean the house every day. It didn't matter how hard I worked at it, she would always yell at me when she came home. Sometimes she would even slap me."

I instruct everyone to take a deep breath. The exercise is over.

Marissa looks at me and asks, "What the heck just happened?"

"We just tricked your Limbic System."

Ed leans forward and says, "Am I right in assuming that her Limbic System thinks I am her mother?"

"Oh, my God, I get nervous when you come home just the way I did when my mother would come home." Marissa addresses me. "My Limbic

System doesn't know the difference between my mom and Ed. Can that be true?"

"What I am saying is that the same thoughts that you had as a little girl are being triggered now. The brain works by association, and you have linked mom and Ed. You are reacting to him the same way you reacted to her because your monkey can't tell the difference. It just knows that this is *the* relationship."

This takes a moment to sink in, and then I continue, "So this thought pattern that you learned at such a young age is controlling your relationship." I look at Marissa and gesture toward Ed. "Ed has the same sort of thing going on inside of him. His monkey thinks you are *that* parent from his past. The monkey is talking to him about it when he interacts with you."

"This can't be true. It seems so fantastic," Ed states.

"So we are in a deep trance. The human condition is in deep trouble, and has been for thousands of years."

"How do we fix it?" asks Marissa.

"This entire process is being driven by thought, *verbal* thought. We are telling ourselves things and reacting to them, and we don't even know we are doing it. If we could clearly see what we are telling ourselves that was getting us off track, the hijacking of the Limbic System would be unmasked. So clearly the problem is *thought*, the voice in your head."

"Yeah?" Ed furrows his brow.

"What if I could show you a simple way of becoming the Master of Thought? So instead of being its slave and doing whatever the monkey tells you to do, you become the master of thoughts that are meant to hijack you and refuse to believe them and be influenced by them?"

"That would be great," says Marissa. "Would it improve our relationship?"

"It will transform it."

CHAPTER 4: THE DARK TRUTH ABOUT THE LIMBIC SYSTEM

There are really only three topics I want to cover regarding the Limbic System: Association, Perception, and Behavior. These are like the Three Musketeers, *all for one and one for all*. Studies of the Limbic System have shown many surprising findings. To a brain scientist this is all fascinating, but to a psychotherapist like me it is horrifying. Most brain scientists know nothing of *psychodynamics*. If they did, they would probably be just as horrified.

The difference between me and most brain scientists is that I have a live person sitting in from of me dealing with real-life problems. Scientists have a brain quivering in a Petri dish. From their more abstract position, the magnitude of their findings might not be completely obvious to them, but it is to me.

Another difference is that a lot of brain research has been done from the standpoint of those with brain lesions where entire areas of the brain have stopped functioning due to damage of some sort. This type of study leads to information about curious deficits and odd behaviors that happen as a result of brain damage. I am not usually looking at someone with brain damage. I am looking at someone whose brain process is out of control but who is generally considered *normal*.

Oh, *psychodynamics*? Psychodynamics is a term that refers, in the vernacular of psychology, to the influence of childhood experiences on adult behavior. The common belief is that there are unconscious emotional forces at work that influence us. These unconscious emotional forces are far bigger than we have ever imagined. In fact, psychodynamics have been shown by research to literally change limbic structures, so much so that they reduce humanity to walking zombies. The hijacking of the Limbic System is so complete, so deep, and so frequent that we have become anesthetized to it. It is the bane of human kind.

One more thing; psychodynamics drives the voice in your head that sounds like you talking to you. We will wind up this chapter talking about the language of the Limbic System.

THE CHAOS OF ASSOCIATION

If you are a man and I say the word "golf," you may think of *green* or the word *club*. If you are a women and I say "skirt," you might think of *short* or polka-*a-dot* (wait a minute, maybe I was the one thinking of *short*). The point is that the brain is a giant association machine. At the heart of that machine is the Limbic System. The brain is constantly analyzing incoming data either from the internal landscape or the external world, and in effect saying, "This is just like that." There is a constant comparison going on that ensures the survival of the organism called "me."

Why the Limbic System? Remember that it is Grand Central Station for emotions in the brain. And since it is wired up so early in life, it stands to reason that our most powerful emotional memories are from those early years. These emotional memories set up inclinations or tendencies to perceive, respond emotionally, and react in a particular way. These inclinations or tendencies have been labeled as "dispositional representations" by brain scientist Antonio Damasio. This means that stored in our brains are tendencies and inclinations to perceive, feel, and behave in a certain way in the near future. In short, our brains are in a state of readiness to deliver up entire reactive patterns, guided by the survival imperatives of the Limbic System at any given moment. Our early conditioning or learning, based on that *first relationship*, sets up many dispositional representations around particular types of associations we might encounter later in life.

These might represent feelings, ways of perceiving, or ways of reacting. The most important of these come in the form of small verbal packets that contain the sense of all of the psychological events that arise in our awareness from those words.

For instance, if the voice in my head says, "I'm in trouble," I will experience what it was like to be in trouble when I was a child and, to a lesser extent, all of the times I have been in trouble ever since. In addition, I will behave or react in the same way. In terms of associations that command the patterns in our life, the most insidious associations come in the form of internal verbalizations. We will look into this in more depth in the chapter on Egocentric speech.

Let me try to sum this up the way I look at the process. During childhood, many dispositional representations are formed, pared back, and rewired to form new patterns. These dispositional representations coalesce around what psychology would call an "issue" or "baggage." This issue gets inextricably linked to a phrase or verbal injunction that triggers behavior that is meant to resolve the issue. We would call this an "emotional reaction." The two most basic of these are related to flight or fight, anger or fear, or predators or prey.

How do these associations work? How does our current experience get hijacked by this reactive pattern? I want to use a metaphor here to try to explain this. Think of our current experience as a baseball and life as the pitcher. The dispositional representation is a very fuzzy and yet extremely stable catcher's mitt. Also, think of the Limbic System as the catcher himself or herself.

So life throws us a pitch. The Limbic system is constantly scanning our experience looking to match our experience with our *issues* so we can defend ourselves and survive. The Limbic System, like a catcher, can only reach so far with its mitt. Not only that, the mitt itself is fuzzy around the edges.

What has to happen is that the ball must become ensnared in enough of the fuzziness in order to be swept into the mitt. The law that governs this is nonlinear dynamics better known as "chaos theory." What we are looking for is a closeness of fit between the ball's trajectory and the glove. Now as the ball slides into the center of mitt, the mitt becomes less and less fuzzy and more rigid and sticky. It is highly unlikely that the ball will bounce out of the mitt.

As the ball settles into the mitt we experience everything associated with having a ball in *that* mitt or whatever emotional issue the Limbic System has associated with that particular mitt.

Not only do we re-experience the feelings and reactions associated with our mitt (issue), but this current experience actually changes the fuzziness of the mitt. So there is adaptation and generalization that tends to shape the mitt to get ready for the next pitch that life throws at us.

That is why there is this sickening repetition to our life experiences. It is as if childhood has doomed us to repeat certain patterns over and over again. What the monkey brain learns in the first 4 to 6 years of life sets a trajectory from which it is extremely hard to deviate. OF COURSE GETTING OUT OF THIS MESS IS THE THEME OF THIS BOOK.

PERCEPTION

Since the monkey is predisposed and has tendencies, perception is preconditioned. The latest research indicates that perception is not some sequential process that happens prior to feelings or behavior. It turns out that we are predisposed by the monkey brain to represent our experience in certain ways and that our five senses and the sensory cortices to which they are linked are therefore primed with expectation and anticipation.

The short explanation of this is that *believing is seeing.* In other words, if my mother rejected me as a child, I will *see* my wife rejecting me in my current experience. If the only tool you have is a hammer, everything looks like a nail.

Thus, perception is simultaneous with emotions and reactions. The process of making meaning out of life and responding to it emotionally is all part of the same gestalt. *Gestalt* is a German word meaning "form" or "shape." It is used in English to refer to the concept of *wholeness.* All of which is governed by the monkey who vigilantly sweeps our current experience at the rate of theta waves (6 times a second or so). This means that we have six chances a second to have the monkey hijack us into seeing something that is not there!

I believe that by combining the work of brain researchers and the linguistic theories of those in childhood development, we find that what binds all of this together is a short, very powerful, internal verbalization – self-talk. We repeat these injunctions to ourselves so often and *for so long* that they have completely faded into the background of the mental cacophony that overwhelms our minds.

There is one more sinister twist to all of this: the system of perception is recursive and reflexive. Since perception is preconditioned and we believe what we expect to see, we then precondition our perception again and loop back through the process. So if my wife says "good morning" to me, I might see that as a form of rejection and react to it accordingly assuming that my wife has some ulterior motive in saying, "good morning." Whatever she does next is also preconditioned in my senses to be rejection, so I again react to rejection.

You know what will eventually happen? She will get sick of all of this and reject me! So perception has a way of becoming a self-fulfilling prophecy. So I fall in love with a series of women who reject me and keep asking myself, "What is wrong with these women?" In fact, life is simply mirroring back my distorted perception. I am the problem!

Behavior and Motives

As if this wasn't overwhelming enough, science has stumbled upon another fact about the Limbic System. All intentional goal directed behavior begins in the Limbic System! In other words the monkey is the gate keeper of motives. This completely flies in the face of the long held belief that decision-making happens in the prefrontal, more adult area, of the brain. There is no question that the prefrontal area is important. It is very much like an inhibitory gate that has the power to squelch the impulses from the more primitive parts of the brain. And I suppose there is some deciding going on there. But my experience is that the prefrontal lobes are an underutilized part of the brain. Or let's say, they are often not put to their best purpose.

What is their purpose? Focus and concentration, memory, anger management, impulse control, but more importantly for our discussion, insight. Anything having to do with thinking about thinking, self-observation, self-referencing or thinking about the thinking of others involves prefrontal activation. When we are paying attention, we are using that part of the brain.

That is all well and good, but the catalyst of goal directed intentional behavior is the Limbic System. There is research that shows when the limbic area of a chicken's brain is disconnected, for instance, the chicken does some occasional pecking, but all purposeful behavior of any kind ceases –even eating.

What this means is that when you *decide* to buy a car, the impulse to do so comes from the monkey. When you *decide* to start an exercise program, the actual synthesis of that goal is prompted by the monkey. It is easy to see that all goal-directed behavior is started by the imperative to make the organism, *me*, benefit from the action in the future. This then is really all about survival and, in that context, it makes a lot of sense.

What happens, according to science, is that the impetus for behavior starts in the Limbic System. The Limbic System reaches out to recruit vast areas of the cerebral cortex. Once this partnership is created, entire hemispheres and huge areas of the brain go into a state of synchronicity and collaborate to carry out the behavior. You might say the brain quivers in co-operation.

Given that childhood development affects limbic structures and that we are in a constant state of influence from our psychodynamics, goal directed, intentional behavior is in big trouble, and thus so are we.

The human condition is the way it is and the world is in the shape it's in because the monkeys are in charge! (My apologies to primates everywhere.)

EGO PATTERNS

So we have all of the pieces in place to understand what I call *Ego Patterns*. The diagram below is completely inaccurate but does serve as a useful roadmap to track down the various aspects of the ego patterns that control our lives, destroy relationships, and get us fired from jobs. I say it is inaccurate in that it is laid out in such a way that it would lead one to believe that the brain processes all of this in sequence. We will see that the process is more simultaneous and later that it is holographic.

Verbal Thought	Perception	Feeling	DefensiveBehavior	Goal/Motive
➡	➡	➡	➡	➡

Figure 5: A linear model of the mind

The voice in your heads speaks. From this comes some meaning out of your current experience. This meaning or perception triggers a feeling like fear or anger, and we defend that painful feeling with a defensive behavior akin to flight or fight. Of course this behavior has a goal or motive such as wanting to be close or be safe. In other words, there is a positive state that we are trying to achieve with our defensive behavior.

From research, we know that the brain is filled with parallel processors nested and looped in millions of ways. What actually happens is more like the diagram below:

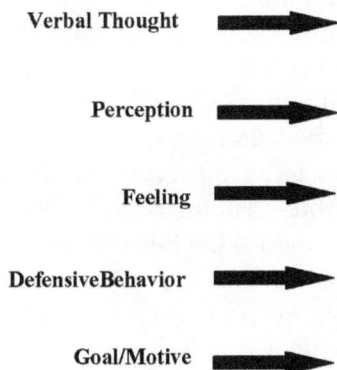

Verbal Thought ➡

Perception ➡

Feeling ➡

DefensiveBehavior ➡

Goal/Motive ➡

Figure 6: A more accurate model of the mind

Who would have thought that perception, feelings behavior and motive were all simultaneous with verbal thought? Ego patterns emerge from the nonlinear dynamics of brain mechanics as a gestalt, an entire state, which takes over the brain. (We will see later that these ego patterns are holographic.) To make this even stranger, research has verified that the motor cortex fires before a person is aware that they have initiated action! It appears there is a ¼ to ½ second delay between action and conscious awareness. It turns out that the brain activates from back to front. If personal awareness is up front in the prefrontal area, then we are nothing more than back seat drivers in our lives! I am always the last to know!

THE LIMBIC SYSTEM AND LANGUAGE

While the Limbic System doesn't speak in well-formed words, sentences, and grammar, it has a language all its own. Brain scientists know that, like so much else in the brain, language is evoked from the limbic system and not from the neocortex. When the neocortex is prodded with electrodes a subject does not start talking. Not so with the Limbic System. Although the adult brain is used to construct, grammatically organize, and sequence the words of language, the source of speech belongs to the monkey brain. When prodded with an electrode, the Limbic System produces emotional cries and warning calls.

"The amygdala made me do it." Perhaps you have heard that saying. The amygdala is like the emotional hub for the Limbic System. For our discussion it is important to note that the amygdala is all about fight or flight and the associations we make concerning danger, survival, and pain. Its job is to keep us moving toward pleasure and away from that which is unpleasant. It does so by pairing our current experience with a catalog of associations left from early childhood development. The amygdala and other limbic structures also become activated when we speak. Even though we might consider the Limbic System nonverbal, it is certainly vocal. In fact, it makes more noise than any other part of the brain. Typically the Limbic System initiates vocalizations involving sexual arousal, anger, and extreme fear.

As the brain grows and develops, the syntax of language becomes wired into the cerebral cortex. But these areas, specialized as they are for verbal communication, are intertwined with the limbic structures that produce emotionally-based grunts, cries and screams. What this means is that adult speech is heavily influenced by the emotional lens of the more primitive structures in the brain.

The Limbic System is primary in perception, meaning making, and expressing the emotional nuances of communication. The amygdala in particular, is largely responsible for the expression and comprehension of not just the babbling talk of an infant, but of adult speech as well.

The auditory neocortex, where the brain produces and decodes language, can be seen as an evolutionary extension of the amygdala. Many brain scientists believe that the language areas have evolved to some extent from the amygdala and remain extensively interconnected with it.

CHAPTER 5: THE EGO MIND

Lisa is telling me the truth about her horrible experiences as a little girl. Her uncle molested her from age seven until she was a teenager. Of course like so many victims, she told her parents and they said to her in effect, "Oh, Uncle Harry wouldn't do anything like that. You must be imagining things."

So Uncle Harry, or whatever his name was, molested her over the years. She had no one to help her. No one would listen or provide protection. Then there were the constant threats of death from Uncle Harry. Helpless children have no alternative than to believe that unless they submit and keep the secret of the abuse, they will be killed.

Now Lisa is left with what every victim of this kind of abuse is left with: vicious thoughts of self-hatred and judgment.

She looks at me through her tears. "I can't help my thoughts. I think everyone hates me. Everyone can see what an evil person I am. I hate myself. I keep telling myself I am no good. I am damaged goods."

"That's completely understandable. Everyone who has ever gone through what you have gone through has the same kind of thoughts."

She looks at me incredulous, "What?"

"Yes," I said. "There are an army men and women who suffer from the same thought patterns as a result of the abuse they went through. Sexual abuse produces a fairly consistent pattern of self hatred and a feeling of exposure. So you are not alone."

"I'm not? I thought I was the only one having these thoughts."

"That is entirely normal. You have to realize that something like one in seven little girls is sexually molested. You have fellow victims literally all around you. Each is suffering in silence, but none know how many of their peers are going through exactly the same thought patterns."

Lisa dabs at her eye with a tissue. "It never occurred to me."

I push the box of tissue closer to her so she doesn't have to reach so far and say, "I am not trying in any way to minimize what you went through. But I do think it is important for you to understand that you have a lot of company. In fact, the level of pain that most people carry is almost unbearable for any of a variety of reasons. But your particular brand of pain is certainly not isolated. It is widespread."

"So what do I do?" she asks.

"Well the traditional approach, from a therapy standpoint, would be to gradually reintroduce the painful memories and feelings so that some kind of healing can take place."

"But I don't want to relive all that bad stuff. I don't want to feel those feelings again," Lisa says firmly.

I lean forward and look her in the eyes, "I never want you to come in here expecting that to happen. This is going to be a safe place, where you are in charge. There is no way I am going to play the role of another abuser in your life by using therapy to inflict pain. And, trust me, forcing you to relive trauma is a form of abuse, no doubt about it."

"Oh, God, I am so glad to hear you say that. I was so worried when I came in here. But I had no other choice. I know I have to do something. My life is a mess."

"Lisa, what if I told you there was a way of overcoming those painful, hateful thoughts? What if I told you there was a way of *mastering* thought instead of being its slave?"

"That would be great. Tell me how."

"Let me ask you, what is the most common thought that you have?"

"'I'm no good.' It is a thought that I have over and over again. 'I'm no good.'"

"Suppose you weren't having that thought, 'I'm no good'?"

Lisa starts to protest. The very idea of being free of that thought is preposterous to her.

"Just go with me and speculate. I am not trying to get you to believe in the impossible. Let's just pretend. Who would you be? What kind of life would you have? How would you experience your day if you didn't have that thought, 'I'm no good'?"

Lisa becomes thoughtful and finally says, "Well I guess I would be happy, at peace."

"Right. So is the fact that you were abused a problem or is the problem your thinking as a result of the abuse?"

She hesitates and says in an asking tone, "My thinking?"

"Of course, without the thought 'I'm no good' you would be free of the pain for the moment and in peace."

I can see that Lisa is skeptical.

I ask her, "So, right now in this moment, is your personal history the problem or is the thought, 'I'm no good,' the problem."

"It's my thinking. My thinking is the problem. But I wouldn't be thinking like this if what happened to me wouldn't have happened."

"Yes, you have a point," I concede. "So let's take a look at someone else and use them as an example."

"Okay," she says with a trace of skepticism in her voice.

"Let me introduce you to George, our example person. George was raised in a violent alcoholic family and was beaten daily by his step father. Today he comes to me and says he can't stay married to his wife because he keeps telling himself that if he gets close to her she will hurt him. Now that makes perfect sense doesn't it?"

"Yes."

"So what is George's problem: the fact that he has a bad personal history or the fact that he believes the thought, 'If I get close she will hurt me'?"

Lisa rubs her face and says, "Okay, okay I get it. Everybody has bad thoughts. Is that it?"

"Not entirely. What I am trying to show you is that everybody has thoughts that come from their early experiences. If we believe our thoughts, we suffer. What I am saying is that the suffering comes from thought not from the origin of the thought. There is this thought, 'I am not okay.' If I believe that thought I suffer. If George believes his thought, he suffers. If you believe your thought, you suffer."

"But I have to believe my thoughts. They are *my* thoughts!" Lisa says a bit exasperated.

"Yes, they are your thoughts, just as my thoughts are my thoughts and George's thoughts are his. But there is something else going on here."

"What's that?"

"Human beings tend to not just believe their thoughts because they're 'my' thoughts. There is another force about thoughts that is far more powerful."

"I don't get it. What do you mean?"

I shift in my chair and pause for a moment. I want Lisa to see this for herself. If I just spell it out for her, she probably won't see it as that important.

"Why do you tend to believe your thoughts?"

"Because they are *my* thoughts." Lisa answers me firmly.

"What you are describing is something I call 'identification.' You are identified with your thoughts."

"Yeah, because they are my thoughts." Now Lisa is sounding a little defensive.

"Okay, so when the voice in your head that sounds like you talking to you says something, you think *that* voice is *you*. Correct?"

"Yeah?"

"What if I told you that the voice that sounds like you talking to you is *not* you?"

"What? What do you mean?"

"I am saying that when we believe our thoughts we suffer, but more importantly you are not your thoughts. More specifically the voice in your head is not you."

"Not me? What the hell is it if it is not me?" Lisa asks in shock.

"It is a function of language and the brain. It is brain talk. It is thinking without a thinker. It is speech without a speaker. Call it the ego mind or the false self."

Lisa looks at me like I am crazy. This will obviously require a bit more explanation.

"Think of it this way. What happens if you eat too many beans or too much broccoli?"

Now Lisa really looks at me like I am crazy. "I get indigestion?"

"Right," I confirm, "you get gas. But you don't form a special relationship with your gas. You just wait for it to pass. You don't say to yourself, 'that's *my* gas.'"

"Okay and your point is .. ?"

"In essence this is what we do with the voice in our heads. Thinking just happens. It is a mechanism, a function of language. It is an Ego mind that loves to talk about itself, look out for itself, and plot to promote itself."

"That's great, but I am telling myself that I hate myself. How is that self-promotion?"

"It doesn't seem like it does it? But let's suppose that pain avoidance is a way of looking out for oneself. Does that sound plausible?"

Lisa nods, "That sounds right."

I look straight into her eyes and ask her, "What pain are you avoiding by telling yourself that you're no good or that others hate you?"

She thinks for a moment and then turns to me with a note of

resignation, "If I tell myself they hate me, I am not hurt if they actually do. Did I get that right?"

"You are right on target. Avoiding pain is about looking out for oneself. But look at me for a moment. I want to have a close caring relationship with you. How am I going to have that if you are telling yourself that I hate you so you don't get hurt?"

"I get it. I'm a mess." Lisa hangs her head and dabs her eyes.

"See, notice that you are doing it again."

Moments later I watch her leave. I notice myself wondering if she will ever want more for her life than what the voice in her head tells her she deserves.

#

I have been going over the relationship between the prefrontal lobes and the Limbic System with Ed and Marissa. And while they are mildly amused, I can see that I better tie this into something that can make a difference in their life so it is not just some abstract idea about the brain.

"So, let's do a little exercise, okay?" They nod in agreement and I go on, "I want you to go inside and silently say your name to yourself."

I watch them carefully, and I can see that they both did that with little effort. "You hear that voice?"

"Yes."

"It sounds like you. It feels like you."

Ed says, "Right . . ."

"It has your tone and timbre. It feels as if it has been there forever." I raise my eye brows. "Yes?"

"I want to explain where that voice comes from."

I settle back into my chair motion at my head. "The right hemisphere and the Limbic System are nonverbal in the grammatical sense. That means that children, before they learn language, are impelled through the world by the nonverbal parts of the brain. So when they walk from one room to the next, action is a function of nonverbal thoughts, cues from the environment, whatever attracts their attention and so forth. Make sense?" I pause to see if Marissa and Ed are tracking this.

"Then at around two or three years of age, children begin to learn language. As their language ability develops, they display two distinctive types of communication. The first is normal social communication. You know, the effort at communicating with another person; 'Hi mommy how are you, when are we going to eat?'"

"The next type of communication has been labeled 'egocentric speech' by researchers in childhood development. " I get up and write "Egocentric Speech" on the board.

"Egocentric speech . . . It seems I've heard of it," comments Marissa. "It seems like I remember that from college."

"Right, if you ever studied childhood development, you may have heard of egocentric speech in connection with Jean Piaget who wrote extensively on the topic."

Ed looks a bit impatient so I move on. "So what is egocentric speech? Well, imagine you are a child and the nonverbal parts of your brain are moving you to run to the backyard. You would use your new found language ability to say out loud, 'I'm running to the backyard.'"

I glance at Ed and say parenthetically, "Hang in there, this all leads to a very important point."

I continue. "Egocentric speech is a commentary spoken by the child out loud to themselves about themselves. That's why it's called 'egocentric.' It is sort of an ongoing commentary on what the child is doing and why he or she is doing it. It is a story – a narrative the child tells to themselves about themselves. This is well documented and all children do this."

I walk to the board and draw the picture of the Limbic System and the prefrontal lobes. This time I insert something in between.

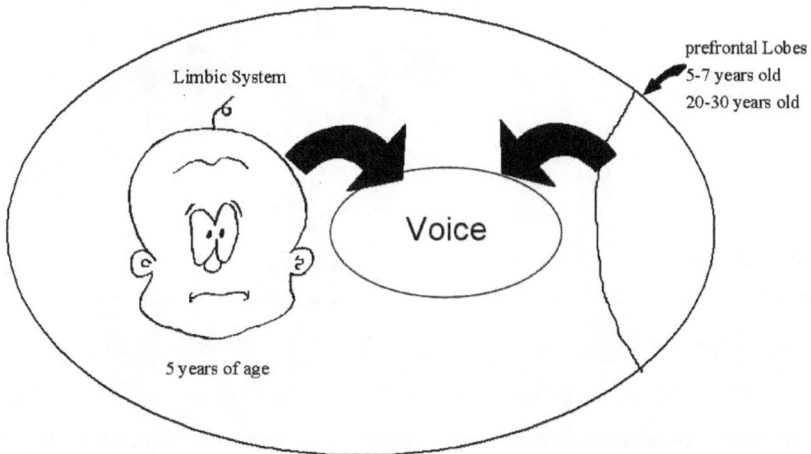

Figure 7: The Voice in your head that sounds like you talking to you.

"At around four or five years of age, we develop the ability to talk to ourselves internally. So what happens is that this 'egocentric speech' goes inside and becomes the voice in your head that sounds like you talking to you. You can see that the Limbic System, the Monkey, and the prefrontal lobes link up and out of this collaboration emerges this internal voice (verbal thought) that takes up a familiar *I* position in our heads."

I finish the diagram by inserting the years that these two parts of the brain fully mature.

Marissa speaks first. "Oh my god! The monkey runs the voice in my head!"

"To a large extent, yes. But there is something that makes this even worse for all of human kind."

Ed asks, "What is that?"

"When this voice goes inside at about four or five years of age, it talks to us about ourselves almost nonstop *for the rest of our lives*. When this happens, we give the voice a label. Do you know what we call it?"

Ed and Marissa are silent for a moment as they think. Finally, Ed pipes up, "Conscience?"

I chuckle, "That is the number one answer I get, but I have an answer that is even simpler than that," I say as I turn and write on the board.

"Me."

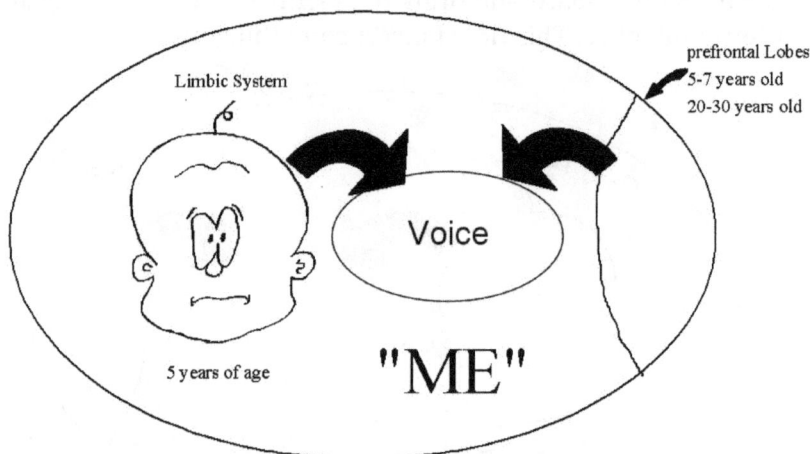

Figure 8: We label the voice in our head that sounds like you talking to you "ME."

I turn back to Ed and Marissa and continue, "We identify the voice in our heads as 'me.'"

Ed looks at the board and looks at me and says, "And this is bad because?"

"It's bad because the voice in your head that sounds like you talking to you is in fact not you."

"It's not?" asks Marissa with a gasp.

"It is thought without a thinker. Speech without a speaker."

Marissa says, "I don't get it. I must be the thinker. They are my thoughts."

"Of course they are your thoughts, just like when you have indigestion it is your gas, right? But you don't identify yourself as your gas, but we do identify ourselves as the voice in our heads."

They are both looking at me like I have lost my mind. I take one hand and grab the other by the wrist. I hold up the hand and shake it. "You don't go around all day saying, 'I'm the hand' do you?"

"No."

"But every time the voice in the head starts up with a verbal thought, there is a sensation that goes with it that tells us that is who we are. Of course the hand is part of you. The voice in the head is certainly a function of *your* brain. But it is not you."

Marissa says, "I think I see what you are getting at."

"Also we have mistaken the voice in the head for something else. Let me prove it to you. Can you tell me where your driver's license is?"

"In my purse" "in my wallet," they say simultaneously.

"Did either of you need to talk to yourself to *know* that?"

Both of them admit that there was no internal dialog that helped them identify the location of their driver's license.

"So we have mistaken the voice in the head for knowledge, wisdom, memory, intuition, and intelligence. It is none of those things."

Ed leans forward and opens his hands, "If it is none of those things, what is it?" He shrugs.

I lean forward playfully mocking his body language. "It is nothing more than a voice in the head. It is a disembodied voice that has no meaning. It is simply the brain talking internally. It is that egocentric speech of a child that has continued through the years. It is an ongoing commentary about you to you and others in an imaginary audience."

Chapter 6: Egocentric Speech

Piaget and Vygotsky

For the voice in your head, 1896 is perhaps the most important year ever. That year two boys were born, one in Switzerland and one in Russia. They were Jean Piaget (1896-1980) and Lev Vygotsky (1896-1934).

Piaget outlived Vygotsky, which may be part of the reason that this book couldn't have been written until today. You see, they had a difference of opinion and perhaps because Piaget outlived Vygotsky, his research and theories of childhood development overshadowed Vygotsky's. This is unfortunate since in one very important aspect of their work, Piaget was wrong and Vygotsky was right. But I am getting ahead of myself.

Piaget was a well-known scientist, but the most important thing that influenced his study of development was the birth of his three children while he was a professor of psychology. His study of the growth and development of his own children was key to his understanding and theories.

As he studied his children he asked one overriding question: How does knowledge grow? His answer was that:

> ... the growth of knowledge is a progressive construction of logically embedded structures superseding one another by a process of inclusion of lower less powerful logical means into higher and more powerful ones up to adulthood. Therefore, children's logic and modes of thinking are initially entirely different from those of adults. (<http://www.piaget.org/biography/biog/html>)

This tends to fly in the face of what we now know about the Limbic

System. In fact, I have noticed that one common theme in the early literature of psychology is the idea that human beings grow and evolve into noble creatures as the years pass. Pshaw!

While Piaget is right that the brain progressively generalizes and integrates an expanded world view, this integration is achieved through the distorted perception of the monkey brain that remains inextricably in charge even into old age.

Piaget's work is known all over the world and is still an inspiration in fields like psychology, sociology, education, epistemology, economics and law. He was awarded numerous prizes and honorary degrees.

Meanwhile Vygotsky was not trained in science but received a law degree from Moscow University. He went on to study literature and linguistics. For Vygotsky, childhood development is mental development -- language and reasoning process. These functions are understood to develop through social interactions with parents.

While Piaget believed that all children go through stages of development, Vygotsky believed that cognitive development was a result of verbal interaction with parents, teachers, and other children. Vygotsky stressed *language dialogue*. For him, children learn and grow by interacting verbally with others through speech. Eventually a child learns to use their own internal speech to direct personal behavior in much the same way that a parent's speech once directed it. The transition from audible speech to internal speech was, for Vygotsky, a developmental process of internalization. At first knowledge exists outside the child, in the environment. Development, as defined by Vygotsky, was gradual internalization, primarily through language, to form adaptation.

Vygotsky, like Piaget, gets carried away with lofty ideas. He believes that we humans are using internalized language for problem solving, to control our behavior and for self-reflection. From my standpoint as a working therapist, this couldn't be farther from the truth. Internal dialogue is a source of mental self-stimulation that we use to justify ourselves, rationalize our mistakes, and to work ourselves into an emotional frenzy over things that are not the least bit important.

Both Vygotsky and Piaget watched young children in problem solving situations talking to themselves out loud. Piaget said speech that resulted in self-directed behavior was *egocentric* and believed it of little importance to children's cognitive development. Vygotsky labeled it as "private speech." He argued that private speech comes from children's interaction with parents and other adults and that through such interactions; they begin to use their parents' instructional comments to direct their own behavior.

While this may be true to some extent, to a much larger extent we all use the voice in our head for other purposes.

EGOCENTRIC SPEECH UP CLOSE

Imagine, if you will, the child's world prior to learning language. Their experience is entirely nonverbal. As we have seen, the entire right hemisphere and the Limbic System are nonverbal. So if the child walks from the house to the backyard, this is prompted by nonverbal thought.

At about 2 to 3 years of age, children begin to learn language. Piaget found that they begin to display two different types of communication at this time. We have alluded to this earlier. Social communication is an effort to talk to another person. But Piaget also observed another type of communication that was distinguishable from social communication in several different ways.

First, he labeled this type of communication as "egocentric" since the child speaks only about him or herself. But also the child does not attempt to place themselves at the point of view of an audience or someone to whom the speech is directed. There is no effort to communicate to anyone, an answer from someone else is not expected, and the child doesn't seem to care if anyone is listening. Egocentric speech is the child talking to him or herself out loud as if they were thinking out loud. In other words, egocentric speech is verbal thought except it is out loud.

Back to the child walking out to the backyard. Once he or she learns language, the egocentric phrase accompanying the trip might be, "Now I am going to the backyard."

What is really important to know about this is that the trip to the backyard is still prompted by nonverbal thought – by the nonverbal parts of the brain. Egocentric speech is nothing more than a commentary. Knowing this is crucial when trying to understand the voice in our heads, which is also a commentary. This child is talking to him or herself about him or herself. As he or she matures, the speech pattern includes ascribing assumed motives and emotions. "I am going to the backyard because I am angry at mommy!" It is as if there must be some reason the nonverbal parts of the brain have me going to the backyard so I am speculating that I am angry at mommy since she won't give me candy.

Piaget observed that egocentric speech decreases as the child gets older and extinguishes itself by the age of seven or eight. Piaget concluded that egocentric speech changed into abstract reasoning. Egocentric talk disappears, he reasoned, because it is useless and therefore dies out essentially at school age.

Vygotsky came to an entirely different conclusion. Interestingly his research showed what we all experience in everyday life; that egocentric speech, like self-talk, nearly doubles when a child is in a stressful situation. Vygotsky clearly saw that children were trying to remedy a situation or solve a problem by talking to themselves about it.

This is exactly what happens to all of us. When we have had a negative encounter or we are up against a difficult problem, the intensity of our self-talk ratchets up in an effort to solve the problem. I believe in both cases the purpose for this is the management of our own internal state. In other words, self-talk, like egocentric speech, is an effort to manage anxiety or guilt or some other intense emotion. We will see later that there is no intelligence in self-talk, so there is, therefore, no problem solving possible from increasing inner speech.

More importantly, Vygotsky concluded that egocentric speech is not extinguished but rather is turned inward. In experiments with older children, Vygotsky found that their silent inner speech had the same basic qualities of egocentric speech. Too bad he didn't do the same experiment with adults. He would have found the same thing! He concluded that all silent thinking is nothing but egocentric speech. Distinct from Piaget, Vygotsky would say that *egocentric speech does not atrophy; it goes underground!*

From my perspective what this means is that the voice in the head that sounds like *you* talking to *you* is the voice of a 5 year old child, driven by the Limbic System. It is a commentary on what you are doing and why are you doing it. It is the left hemisphere watching the right hemisphere's activity, trying to make sense out of it, and turning it into a narrative we might label "my story."

In his book, *Thought and Language*, Vygotsky concludes:

"Our experimental results indicate that the function of egocentric speech is similar to that of inner speech: It does not merely accompany the child's activity, it serves mental orientation, conscious understanding; it helps in overcoming difficulties; it is speech for oneself, intimately and usefully connected with the child's thinking. Its fate is very different from that described by Piaget. Egocentric speech develops along a rising, not a declining, curve; it goes through an evolution, not an involution. In the end, it becomes inner speech." (1986, p. 286)

THE GAME-SHOW-HOST IN YOUR HEAD

Many of you reading this may be too young to remember an American icon of sports casting named Howard Cosell. "I'm telling it like it is," he would say about his style. I remember Howard Cosell as an irritating, grating, and raspy reminder of what one's ego mind might sound like who would drone on and one in a nasally tone that made you want to turn down the TV. My apology to Howard Cosell fans the world over.

My point about Cosell is that whenever the man opened his mouth you knew it was Howard Cosell. There was no way to deny the tone, timbre, and quality of his voice. At sporting event after event, his unmistakable voice could be heard and heard and heard.

We all have our own sports caster, game-show-host in the head.

Meanwhile, Vygotsky concludes that in adults there is no connection between linguistic process (the game-show-host) and nonverbal thought. Clearly there are vast areas of thought that have no direct relationship to speech. Investigation into thought, during Vygotsky's tenure, had proven that much of thought functions without word images. In fact, Vygotsky's writing makes it clear that inner speech has no relationship to intellect. Then he stuns the world by suggesting that animals, like my cat Ronnie, probably have intelligence similar to humankind; they simply have no verbal thought.

So what is this voice in the head? It is a commentary as I have said. Let's consider what a commentator does. He interprets what is happening and then dishes up a version of it for general consumption. He explains. He interprets. He cajoles. He rationalizes. He ascribes motives that are not the real motives.

"Ladies and genetlemen. There is no way Mark would have verbally abused his wife. She must have done something to have prompted it. He's not a bad person. He works hard. He only goes to the bar once a week..." And on and on and on.

Egocentric speech becomes egocentric inner speech, i.e. verbal thought. It has the inner voice of an adult, or whatever age you are. It sounds like you. It has your tone and timbre. But it is essentially a five-year-old since it has a functional relationship to the Limbic System. And when we identify it as *me*, it becomes the source of all emotional and psychological suffering.

But it is nothing more than a game-show-host that lives in the head masquerading as *me*. It is a commentary which means it is always *after the fact*. It is egocentric which means is drives us to think of ourselves and no one else. It is interested in survival which means you all must die so I can live.

The games-show-host is the monkey. It is not intelligent and yet we have mistaken it for knowing, intelligence, intuition, wisdom, and decision making. It is none of these things.

I drove by a car the other day. As I did I became aware of a powerful affinity that I had for the hubcaps on that car. There was just something about them. They were sharp-looking, shiny, classic. As I became aware of these hubcaps and how attractive they were, the voice in my head said, "I really like those hubcaps!"

So what happens is we *know*, we see the big picture, we experience resonance, we become aligned with truth, knowledge is revealed and a split second later the game-show-host in our heads speaks up and tries to take credit for it. Like a politician who finally has to explain the way they voted and says, "Well, I voted for it before I voted against it."

The inner voice is egocentric. It rationalizes, makes excuses, shifts blame, and obfuscates. It loves the story, its expertise is drama. It lives in a little tiny, constricted world: a world of escape, anger, retaliation, and justification.

But there is good news. The voice in your head that sound like *you* talking to *you* is *not you*!

Chapter 7: Witness Thought Transformation™

O kay, Duncan, it's time to become the *Master of Thought*. Are you ready?"

"As ready as I'll ever be." Duncan digs his hips into the chair as if I am going to deliver a body blow instead of a dose of insight.

"Now wait for the next thought. . . It is going to be an internal verbalization like, 'what if I don't have a thought?'"

"Oh my gosh, that was the thought I just had," he smiles as if to say, how did you know that would be the next thought?

"Or the next thought might be; 'what's the *right* thought,' or 'what thought am I supposed to have?' A lot of people also have a thought along the lines of, 'I'm not going to do this right.'"

"Okay."

"Just wait for the voice in your head to speak. It is always speaking." I look at Duncan and see that his attention is turned inside. "When you become aware that you are having a thought, just notice it. Notice that you are thinking. Don't pay any attention to the content of the thought. What you are trying to do is become aware that thinking is happening, that the *thought process* itself is taking place."

"Then what am I supposed to do?"

"Just notice that the voice in your head is speaking and become aware of it; 'Oh, I'm having a thought.' 'Oops, there is another one.'"

Duncan looks at me with a blank stare. "I am not getting this."

"Try this. Have you had lunch today?"

Duncan looks at me and then his brows go up. "Oh, uh no."

"Alright, observe your stomach and tell me if you are hungry."

Duncan shifts his eyes down and to the middle. "No, I am not hungry."

"Now, observe your mind and tell me if you are thinking." I pause and then say, "And when you notice the voice in your head, what does it do? What happens to the thought when you try to observe it?"

Duncan is deep in thought for a moment and turns to me. "It stops. The voice just goes away."

"Right," I say gleefully. "When you try to directly observe the process of thought, the mind goes quiet."

Duncan is looking a little startled as if that was the last thing he expected to discover. His look turns from quizzical to concerned and then back to quizzical. I wait until he seems through processing what he just observed before I speak up: "Duncan, let me ask you a question."

"Okay," he answers quietly.

"When the voice in your head stopped, did you die?"

Duncan looks at me like I am crazy. "No."

"So you are not the voice in your head. That is not who you are. If you can observe the voice and the voice stops, that voice cannot be you. Does that make sense?"

"Oh, my gosh. I have never thought of it that way."

A long silence ensues while I let Duncan take this all in. Finally he looks at me and asks, "If I am not the voice in my head, who am I?"

"Good question, Duncan. Let's leave that for a while. There are many other things to discover. First, I want to teach you a practice that will lead to personal transformation."

"Okay, let's do it."

"You just did the core of the practice I have named *Witness Thought Transformation™*. It involves merely watching your thoughts. When you watch a thought, it stops. When you witness thought, it transforms."

"Oh, I see, witness thought transformation™, cute."

"Right, catchy. Now let's try again. Wait for the next thought to appear in your mind. It is going to be your own internal voice saying something, anything. Then merely turn your attention to it and observe the voice in your head that sounds like you talking to you."

Duncan takes a moment to go inside and then says, "It stops. You've got to be kidding me. When I try to observe *me* talking to *me*, I can't."

"Right. This is an exercise in awareness. It turns out that you cannot talk to yourself and be aware of it at the same time."

Duncan looks shocked and looks at me, "Why is this happening?"

I get up and draw my, by now familiar, diagram of the brain (figure 5).

"Notice that it takes the prefrontal lobes in concert with the Limbic System to generate the voice in your head."

"Right . . ."

"Remember when we first talked about the prefrontal lobes, I told you that we use the prefrontal lobes for focus and attention. So when you are paying attention, you are activating that part of the brain."

Duncan raises his eyebrows. "Yes, and I believe you said that people who have attention deficit disorder often have deficits in their prefrontal area."

"Yes, that is correct. Now consider these two functions that the prefrontal lobes must perform. First it is inextricably involved in generating the internal voice. It is also heavily involved when we need to pay attention."

"Okay," says Duncan, "that all makes sense to me."

I turn to the drawing and point to the diagram. "It turns out that the prefrontal lobes can't do these two things at once. So when you pay attention you cannot talk to yourself."

"Oh, I get it. It's like we can't walk and chew gum at the same time."

"Yes, but the implication of this is huge. What this means is that when we are talking to ourselves, we are not paying attention."

Duncan looks from me to the diagram and then back to me. "And this is a problem because?"

"When we are paying attention, we are present. What are we present for? Life. The only way we actually show up for Life is when we are paying attention. When we are talking to ourselves, we are paying attention to the egocentric babble that goes on all of the time."

"Boy, I know that's true."

"What this really means is that we are not *living* Life, we are *thinking* life."

Duncan nods as he takes this in.

"Duncan, it is as if you and I went to a football game. You are sitting there taking in the smell of the fall air, the sounds and the colors of the people in the stands, the pageantry of it all. You are watching the game, the teams, and the strategy.

"Meanwhile, I am sitting next to you with a set of earphones on. I am listening to the broadcast of the game on the radio. Which one of us is actually experiencing the game?"

Duncan thinks for a moment and says, "I am."

"Right, I am experiencing the *commentary* about the game. I am experiencing the game through the filter of the commentator's perspective and interpretation."

"Of course, I get it."

"This is what happens to all of us. We live most of the time in a world of mental abstraction. And we have become so mesmerized by the sound of our internal voice that we are hopelessly inured. And, no matter what Life gives us, we are not ready to be unplugged from the headphones."

I can see that Duncan is considering the implications of this in his own experience.

"Of course, the sad fact is that the commentator is so often the *monkey-brain*. So the internal dialogue is heavily influenced by whatever happened to the child in the first five years. The dialogical self may sound like a real glib orator, but more often than not it is a hurt, angry, fearful five-year-old."

"Okay, Doc, so what is this practice you want me to do?" Duncan looks like he has had the realization that so many do when they piece all these facts together.

"Alright, so the core of the practice you already know. I want you to try to catch yourself thinking. You notice the voice in your head and it stops. You become lost in thought and you wake yourself and realize you are thinking. The voice in your head that sounds like you talking to you starts up, you catch it and it stops. Try it again right now."

Duncan turns inward for a moment and then nods. "This is really amazing. Who would have thunk it? No pun intended."

"Now that we have established that, there are three things that are of utmost importance. First, we are not trying to *stop* the thought. We are not trying to make the voice go away. This is an exercise in Awareness. It just so happens that when you are paying attention, the voice stops. Think of it as a little boy trying to get a cookie out of the cookie jar. Every time he reaches for a cookie, you are vigilant and you spot him, so he pulls his hand back right away. So number one, we are not trying to stop the thoughts."

"If we are not trying to stop them, what are we trying to do?" asks Duncan.

"We are making them irrelevant. A thought is just a thought. It is a spontaneous product of the brain making associations in language. We are the Awareness that is witnessing the thought. A thought is just a function. It is not who we are. As you practice Witness Thought Transformation™, this will gradually dawn on you. So we are putting thought in its place by watching it."

Duncan nods and I continue, "So we are not trying to stop the thoughts. It just so happens that when we become aware, thought stops.

"Okay secondly, we are not trying to substitute *good thoughts* for *bad thoughts.* The problem is *thought* itself. We have mistaken ourselves for thought. We are trying to break the spell of mistaken identity. Having better thoughts without changing this mistake leaves us sound asleep with better thoughts."

"So you are not a proponent of *positive thinking*?"

"No, I am a proponent of being *conscious*, not thinking better. Plus, whoever thought that you could stop negative thinking without learning to watch all of your thoughts? Using Witness Thought Transformation™ you will begin to see even subconscious thoughts that have been there all of your life."

"Man that would be great."

"Okay, so we are not trying to stop thought, and we are not trying to substitute good thoughts for bad thoughts. So here is the last rule of thought watching. Practice this on the *small* thoughts."

"What do you mean small thoughts?"

"I mean the simple, everyday, meaningless, mundane, day dreamy, kind of thoughts we have when we are just driving along or in the shower. By the way, I missed one rule. Do this when you are *alone*. In the car is a perfect place to practice Witness Thought Transformation™. The voice is always talking, isn't it?"

"You got that right."

"So do this around the small thoughts about the weather, about the football team, the tooth paste. Just try to catch yourself engaging in internal dialogue"

Duncan frowns and asks, "Why the small thoughts? I would have thought you would go after those hairy, thorny thoughts around all of the problems in life."

"Yes, it sounds counter intuitive. But when you think about it, it makes perfect sense. We are trying to awaken from the dream that we are the *thinker*. Thinking just happens. When you start introducing problems, emotions, reactivity and defensiveness into the practice, it is just too much to deal with. After all, this is a *practice*, a practice that leads to a transformation in Awareness. Then we can tackle all of those other things with a powerful new tool from a higher level of consciousness.

"Since Witness Thought Transformation™ is a practice, we start on the practice field – those small thoughts."

I send Duncan on his way, knowing that until I see him again, he will struggle a bit with the practice. I am ready to help him take this step. It usually takes a week or two for someone to *get it*. But I know that if they actually do the practice it will only take a day or two.

I look at my schedule and see that Ed and Marissa are in the next time slot.

#

Ed looks at me and asks, "Now why am I doing this again?"

"Remember at our first session you said you wanted to get the most out of your relationship with Marissa?"

"Right."

"It turns out that what Einstein said was absolutely true, 'No problem can be solved from the same consciousness that created it. We must look at the world anew.' Witness Thought Transformation™ gives us a new set of eyes. With awareness, you will be able to see things in a new and different way. You will literally move to a higher level of consciousness. So you will not only see your relationship in a new way, but you will see the entire world in a new way."

Ed says, "Okay, I understand. I just thought that therapy meant that you endlessly talked about the drama until you got it right."

"Oh, Ed," Marissa chides.

"I can certainly understand that. That is the image that therapy has all right. But Witness Thought Transformation™ really isn't therapy. Every now and then I get in trouble with people because they want to talk endlessly about the problem, as if that is magically going to solve it. Of course, what it really means is that they don't want to solve the problem. They just love reviling in the drama."

Marissa looks at me and asks, "Could you go over the practice again? By the way, why do you call it Witness Thought Transformation™?"

"Let me answer that by having you do the practice. Now just wait for the next thought. It is going to be the voice in your head that sounds like you talking to you. Then just merely observe the fact that the voice is there. Pretend that it is a news anchor in your head instead of yourself. When you become aware of it, the moment you become aware of it, what does it do?"

I can see her turning inside to watch her thought. "It goes away. It always goes away when I try to become aware that it is there."

"Right, so you are witnessing the thought. When you do that it transforms, it stops, and in a very real sense, you transform too. We transform because we learn that we are not that voice."

Ed leans forward. "Wait a minute. If I take this whole idea one more step it seems you are leading us to the radical notion that life would go one just fine if the voice was not there. That the voice in my head is not the deliberator or the chooser or the doer, the one who initiates action, but rather is always a commentator after the fact."

"Right, that is exactly right!" I laugh and they both get sort of a shocked look. "Imagine it is 3 am and you just wake up enough to go to the bathroom. Is there a *doer* that initiates the trip to the toilet? Do you lie there and tell yourself 'I better get up'?"

"I never looked at it like that."

"What I am telling you is that action happens – life happens. We tell ourselves about it a fraction of a second later as if to take credit for it. This has actually been confirmed in studies. Our awareness that we have *decided* on some action takes place a fraction of a second after action has been initiated."

"Wow, I thought I was in control," states Marissa.

"Well, the part of you that thinks it is in control is most definitely not in control of anything but a commentary about control."

"Okay," Marissa starts up, "if what you are saying is true then what about important insights and internal processing? Won't they be shut off if I do this practice? It makes me anxious to think about missing something."

"Not at all. Let's make a distinction here. Internal processing and insight is not verbal. Then there is the talking we do about internal insights. If you study your mind, you see clearly that the internal 'me' that talks in your head is not the source of knowing, intuition, intelligence or anything of the kind. It has been masquerading all of our lives as that source however."

CHAPTER 8: WITNESS THOUGHT TRANSFORMATION™ REDUX

THE TRUE PURPOSE OF THE VOICE IN YOUR HEAD

Now that we have completely exposed the dialogical self as a faker, a miscreant, the *ego mind* that it is, now that we have blown the myth that there is a *me* that lives in the head - what's to be done with it, this voice in the head?

Think of Descartes. In the 17th century Descartes concluded that he could be certain that he existed because he had thoughts. "Thinking is our essence as it is the only thing about us that cannot be doubted," he said. Descartes defined thought as "what happens in me such that I am immediately conscious of it, insofar as I am conscious of it."

Descartes posited a "little man" behind the eyes to process visual stimuli. The word "homunculus," meaning little man, refers to a functioning system thought to be run by a "little man" that lives inside your head. You know that little *me* that sounds like you talking to you? This homunculus is an inner entity or agent that is somehow assumed to be in our brains, making things run. One example of this is Descartes' use of the homunculus to resolve his theory of dualism, that the soul and the body are two completely separate entities.

What we have done so far is to annihilate the whole idea of a homunculus by identifying its source in the Limbic System. The inner voice is of no use, it interferes, it interprets, it commentates. What's worse is that this is all through the filter of the Limbic System – a hurt, angry, fearful five-year-old.

But wait. Is the *voice*, like a set of tonsils, a constant source of irritation until cut out and cast away? Could it be that the voice is like a useless mass of lymphoid tissue that has no discernable use? Actually, no.

So of what value is the internal dialogue, this speaker in search of an interlocutor? The answer is found in what it is. It is a voice; it uses language. So the inner voice that sounds like me talking to me is a function of language and as such has a use restricted to language.

For instance, as I am writing these words, I am spontaneously talking to myself on the inside. In other words, I am dictating the words internally as I am writing them or typing them on my computer. I am using language. Or when I am reading, unless I am a speed reader, I am sub-vocalizing the words in my mind. Again, I am using language.

Let's say you invite me over to your house for dinner. As I drive to your house, I might be repeating the directions in my head, "Let's see, I go down Main Street and turn left on Elm Street," and so forth. Again, I am using language to reinforce my short-term memory.

So the voice in your head has one main purpose: to process language. All the rest of the commentary, reassurance, rationalizations, and rehearsal serve no real purpose whatsoever.

THE PRACTICE OF WITNESS THOUGHT TRANSFORMATION™

The practice of Witness Thought Transformation™ is amazingly simple, and yet the mind wants to make it very complex. And it's the simplicity of it that allows it to work. As a matter of fact, believe it or not I just had a client who canceled on me because he thought I was too crazy. He thought that watching his thoughts was just not going to solve his relationship problems, so he's down the road looking for another therapist.

When I started doing counseling with couples, I began to see a pattern, and that pattern later became a book that I wrote called *The Dance of the Lion and the Unicorn*. As I worked with people over the years I realized that really what people needed to do was watch their thoughts, so I started teaching them how to do exactly that. In some cases it was very successful, but in a lot of cases it wasn't particularly successful at all. I would wonder, "Why is this not working?"

After a while it occurred to me the reason why it wasn't working for so many people, and I don't mean to insult anybody when I say this, but literally people did not know what a *thought* was. When I explain to people that a thought is the voice in your head that sounds like you talking to you, all of a sudden the lights go on and people transform. Remember, the voice in your head that sounds like *you* talking to *you is not you*. When you realize that fact on a moment-by-moment basis in your life, you awaken and you literally do have an awakening experience. For some people this may come as a bolt of lightning, for some people it's an awakening that occurs over the course of days or weeks, or sometimes it literally happens in my office. As I'm explaining this, people *realize* the truth, and they just automatically go to a higher level of consciousness. I've seen this happen over and over again. And of course for many people who have struggled for 10, 20 years or more pursuing enlightenment and higher consciousness and the like, this has been the missing idea that they needed along the way.

One of my students recently said this:

> "I am a meditator and I'm a great admirer of writers such as Tolle, Adyashanti and Michael Brown. I was introduced to Mark Waller's work by a former T.M. (see glossary) teacher, and within 2 weeks I had a profound shift in awareness. Mark's Witness Thought Transformation™ teaching gives the mechanics of enlightenment in the most accessible way, and a practice that rapidly shifts consciousness. So many people can tell you of the view from the mountain top, but Mark shows you the route to climb."

Let me review the fundamentals of Witness Thought Trans-formation™. It's very simple. You're going to wonder why nobody ever thought of this before.

What I want you to do is just sit there and wait for the next thought to occur in your mind. The next thought might be "I'm not going to do this right." "What if I don't have a thought?" "What's the *right* thought to have?" "What is this some kind of a game?"

The idea is to separate yourself from the voice in your head and just observe the thinking process. Now let me repeat the metaphor I used earlier. What I'd like you to do is merely observe your stomach and notice if you're hungry. What I want you to do is use that same power of observation and observe your mind and notice if you're thinking. The instant that you observe your mind thinking, notice what happens to the voice in your head.

What you'll find when you try to witness thought itself is that you're witnessing the process of thought and not getting involved in each thought. You're not paying any attention to the content of thinking. So when the voice in your head starts talking, separate yourself from the thought and just observe the fact that you're experiencing a thought. The instant that you observe the thought, it stops and everything goes quiet. Now it may only happen for a fraction of a second and then the stream of thoughts starts up again. But that's an opportunity for you to stand back again and observe the fact that you're having another thought, remembering that a thought is the voice in your head that sounds like you talking to you.

When you try to observe thought, the voice stops. Then it will start right back up again. It usually changes subject when it starts again but it will start up again. You merely observe it again and the voice stops again. You will find that you cannot actually observe your own self-talk.

Using the practice of Witness Thought Transformation™ you will discover that when you're the *witness* of thought, the thought *itself* transforms. You are *not* your thoughts; you're the observing awareness that's watching the thought. Every time we see the thought stop the idea comes into our head, "Wait a minute, I'm here still watching and the thought has stopped, so obviously I'm not that voice in my head." When that idea completely takes over through the practice of Witness Thought Transformation™, you do experience an awakening and you start looking at the world through a whole new set of eyes.

THE RULES OF THE ROAD

Let me give you the rules to follow for Witness Thought Transformation™. Some of these feel counterintuitive, and it doesn't matter how often I say them or how strongly I say them, people seem to ignore what I'm saying. So it would be a really good idea to write these down and refer back to them.

Here are four extremely important things that make this work. If you don't follow all of them, the practice won't work:

1. You are not trying to stop the thoughts.

It just so happens when you observe *thinking* the thought stops all by itself. So we're not attempting to stop our thoughts. After I've trained someone to do this, they'll often come back the next week and say, "Well no matter what I do I can't stop the thoughts." Again, you're not trying to stop the thoughts. You cannot *tell* or force the ego mind to stop, but when you simply observe the ego mind, it stops dead in its tracks and you go into an ensuing silence and a stillness that you are able to observe when the thought stops. So number one, you're not trying to stop the thoughts.

2. You are not trying to substitute good thoughts for bad thoughts.

The problem is *thought* itself. We mistakenly believe ourselves to be the *thinker*. We are not the thinker. Thinking just happens. We have a disembodied voice in our heads being generated by the brain and we have mistaken that voice for ourselves and that's where all the trouble comes from. So it's not about the fact that we're having negative thoughts as opposed to positive thoughts. After all, how can you ferret out your negative thoughts if you don't learn how to watch all of your thoughts? So you're not trying to substitute good thoughts for bad thoughts; the problem is thought itself. For those of you with any kind of a background in the New Testament, in Second Corinthians 10 Paul says, "hold in captivity every thought." He doesn't say "every bad thought"; he says, "every thought." So that's rule #2.

3. Practice on the small thoughts.

This also feels counterintuitive. This is a practice. I want you to use the most inconsequential, easy, simple thoughts there are to watch. What are those? "Oh it's time to get more toothpaste. I'm almost out." "Wait a minute I've got to stop and get gas before I go home." "I wonder if it's going to rain tonight or if the rain will start tomorrow."

Those kinds of internal dialogues are all inconsequential. There's no emotional loading to them, and they are the easiest ones to practice on. Do not practice Witness Thought Transformation™ on the stressful thoughts, the thoughts that have a lot of emotional impact. Don't practice when you're with somebody else, especially somebody you're in conflict with. It just simply won't work that way. What you want to do is practice on the thoughts that are the simple, day dreamy, everyday, ordinary thoughts that just occur when you're standing in front of the mirror or when you're driving in your car or any number of other mundane situations.

4. Do the practice when you're alone.

You're in the shower, you're in the car, and maybe you're in a work environment where you're working alone. You're trying to catch yourself thinking. That's all you're doing. Every time you catch yourself thinking, the thinking stops and you awaken a little more. Eventually that Awakening is permanent.

I happen to think that driving in the car is perfect. There is no one there but you and the voice in your head. What better time to catch yourself thinking?

Now that I have covered the rules, let me address some of the most common pitfalls to doing the practice of Witness Thought Transformation™. Recently I had a conference call where these came up. Let me share the transcript of the call with you.

Q: One of the problems I have had in trying to be observant of my thoughts as *things* is that I find my mind going quiet. Now while I'm expecting that a quiet mind is what I want to be achieving, I don't find it in any way a positive thing. I just find myself stalling, becoming ineffective.

Dr. Mark Waller. Okay so here's one of the pitfalls that I run into all the time. We are so driven and we're such achievers and we're so looking for results that what happens is somebody will do the practice, they'll observe their internal voice, and the voice will stop. Then the ego mind comes in and says, "That's it?" See, you have to repeat the process over and over again until you "get it."

Q: And by *get it* I assume, and I don't want to put words in your mouth, but I assume you kind of shut the ego mind questioning up for good.

Dr. Mark Waller. Well, the ego mind questioning about the practice is like the thief dressing up like a police officer to help catch the thief. What happens oftentimes when we do the practice is we do the practice and then the voice comes back and starts talking to us about doing the practice and that's how problems manifest.

Q: Yeah, I've been there.

Dr. Mark Waller. And so what you do with that is you just notice, "Oh, I'm talking to myself again." You just bring yourself back to awareness and you notice, "Oh, that was another thought." Don't allow yourself to play that circular game anymore. Realize that the ego does not want to die here, it's under attack and it has to come up with some philosophy to plug into this thing that sabotages it and that's exactly what it is doing: saving itself.

Q: And it's a very clever thing. Just by default it's a very clever thing and it's hard to outwit it. It is funny just talking about it as a *thing* but anyway that was my question. Thank you.

Dr. Mark Waller. Well I hope I answered it for you.

Q: Yes indeed.

Dr. Mark Waller. Yeah, just stay with the practice and *witness* all the ancillary thoughts that come along questioning the practice. That's natural, what you're experiencing happens all the time. It's really important to me that you understand how to do this practice.

Q: I have a question. So what happens when we stop trying to manipulate everything either bodily or mentally?

Dr. Mark Waller. What happens if you try to stop manipulating it?

Q: That's correct.

Dr. Mark Waller. Well, the belief originally was that if you manipulated life you could get an outcome, and that's never been the case. See, the ego wants to believe it's in control of something, so it's desperately trying to anticipate the next moment all the time. Instead of actually being present in the moment, we're trying to anticipate the moment, and by anticipating, we take ourselves out of *presence*. So we never really live. We're *thinking* about the next moment all the time and never actually experiencing the moment itself. What you find is that life without thought goes on quite normally and quite naturally. It doesn't need our interference with it at all. We have the false belief that unless we mess with life it's not going anywhere productive and that's simply not true.

Q: So if a person's in some circumstances that they find unfavorable they should not try to manipulate it?

Dr. Mark Waller. See we're really talking about two things here. We're talking about the practice of Witness Thought Transformation™. We're not talking right now about struggling against the situation that we don't like. It doesn't matter what situation you're in right now. Eventually you're going to have an internal dialogue about going to the grocery store aren't you?

Q: That's right yes.

Dr. Mark Waller. Okay, so practice on those thoughts and, for now at least, forget about the unfavorable circumstances. See, this is the other pitfall, and I really appreciate the fact that you brought this up. People are so dedicated to struggling with their problems that they won't listen to the instructions to do the practice. They'll come back on the second call or the next time in my office and say, "yeah but I still have a problem."

I say, "Well you know that's too bad, you've got a problem. We're talking about a practice that's going to set your mind free here, are you willing to do the practice?"

"No, I'm not willing to do it I just want to solve my problem."

And basically that's the answer the ego gives. So your unfavorable circumstances don't change, but you know there are ways to deal with that that we can talk about, but Witness Thought Transformation™ literally gives you a new set of eyes to see the circumstances from a much more powerful perspective and you're not going to get there unless you do the practice the simple way the way I'm telling you to do it.

That's a great question. I really appreciated that because that's the kind of thing that sidetracks people every single day as I teach this. It's more difficult to get away from our insistence that we want life to be different than it is and just try to focus on something that's actually going to help us. I really understand how difficult it is not to become ensnared in those things. And even as we're reaching out to learn something new we just can't even learn it because we're just so obsessed with the bad feelings and the difficult circumstances that we believe we have.

Q: Mark, you said I'm not trying to stop the thoughts. Does that mean that the more we do the practice, the longer the intervals between thoughts will be? Is that one of the ways that you can tell that you're doing it, - well okay you said not to ask about doing it right - but I am.

Dr. Mark Waller. Ha ha. You know what you're describing actually does happen, but I don't tell people that because then they're going to be focused on that and that's exactly what I don't want you to do. I don't want you to focus on a *result*. I want you to just do the practice the way I've described because it works like magic. And you will find that you're going to get something even more blessed and glorious than stopping thoughts or having a quieter mind; you're actually going to be able to *live*. And so when you're actually living and you're not a slave to the voice in your head any longer, you don't care if the voice is there or not. It's not an issue. But if you focus on getting it quiet or getting a result and getting it to stop, then it just sabotages the whole process. So that's a great question that you brought up because that's the thing that trips people up all the time. So far we're hitting all of the important questions. It's really amazing. Did that help?

Q: Yeah, thank you.

Dr. Mark Waller. So don't look for a result, just do the practice the way I'm telling you to do it and just don't look for a result.

Q: Okay.

Dr. Mark Waller. Just kind of take it on faith. Imagine that you've got an intruder living in your head and it's disguising and using your voice. What you're trying to do is to spot this guy. And every time he speaks with your voice you want to just spot him, catch him.

Q: I really appreciate what you're saying about just focusing on grocery questions and things like that because ever since I read your book I have been trying to use it in the midst of a heated argument with my husband: "don't listen to the thought, don't listen to the though." I've got little notes up saying "Watch your thoughts, watch your thoughts." So I really appreciate that that's going to help a lot. Yeah, it's been wonderful, even the misuse of it that I've been doing.

Dr. Mark Waller. And you know I don't mean to condemn people who are trying to watch their thoughts in the middle of an argument but it's kind of like trying to scale a cliff. You know I'm giving you a path up the mountain that's very easy. If you want to scale a cliff go ahead but I've got this other path here that doesn't take much effort. Would you rather take the hard way up?

Q: No I prefer the non-effort way, so thank you.

Dr. Mark Waller. Alright these are great questions. Anybody else?

Q: I guess I have a bit of a comment. I know that sometimes when men and women are talking, men have to be the problem solvers and women just want someone to listen to them. Maybe sometimes people put themselves into that masculine perspective of "oh it must be solved."

Dr. Mark Waller. Okay great. And you know you might want to know, I don't look at any of this particularly through the lens of gender. I don't find gender to be helpful in this work at all and so even my Lion and Unicorn theory does not track gender. But you're making a great observation there how we can be unhelpful by just following certain tendencies we're acculturated to.

CHAPTER 9: SPEECH WITHOUT A SPEAKER

Duncan is leaning back in his chair recapping for me his first week of thought watching. What I am looking for in the first week is that people try the practice of Witness Thought Transformation™ just enough to get the hang of it so we can move to a more in-depth view of it. But it does seem to take a few days of *orientation*. Then we can have a better discussion about it.

"I continue to have conversations in my head because I am afraid I won't be able to problem solve and survive without them."

"Yes, there is this illusion that the ego-mind gives us that we have some control over what is happening and that we need to mull it over in our mind. But what really is happening is that the brain processes the problem and tries it on by projecting the feeling of it into the body. Getting a gut feeling is really part of the process since the body in a very real sense is the theater of the mind. Verbal thought has absolutely nothing whatsoever to do with this process. Once we have come to a nonverbal conclusion, then we talk about it in our heads as if this voice is something profound, and convince ourselves that any wisdom we are experiencing is coming from the internal dialogue."

"The other thing I noticed is that I can claim that I believe in living in the moment and spontaneously do what I am inclined to do in the moment, but in actuality I still keep talking to myself to survive. I call this 'decision making,'" Duncan said.

I chuckle, "Right, there is this popular misconception that we make decisions with the front or adult part of the brain. In fact what really happens is that the decision gets made by the Limbic System which hijacks the cerebral cortex and then we justify it by talking to ourselves."

"The monkey – it all goes back to the monkey," says Duncan shaking his head. "I have also noticed that I converse with myself when I am alone for entertainment. Sometimes I laugh or cry like I'm a character in a play. After that, I notice the dialog and it stops! I can remember doing this when I was very little. I spent time alone, which required that I entertain myself. "

I remember Duncan telling me that he was the youngest in his family and this reminds me of someone else's experience. "I had a client once who was an only child, and he said very much the same thing. It seems as if that kind of isolation breeds a dependence on the internal dialogue. It seems to be self-soothing."

"That is exactly my experience," states Duncan. "Now I have a question. If your instruction is that we are not trying to stop thought, does that mean we should be in a constant state of watchfulness? I have tried that and it stops thought entirely, but it becomes a real effort. Or are you saying we should watch the thought, the thought stops and then watch the next that arises? Even though that may mean that from one moment to the next we have to start watching again. So it's not a steady stream of alertness but rather a consistent jumping in, right?"

"Yes. It is a lot like cockroaches in the kitchen. They scramble when you turn on the light. What we are practicing is *turning on the light*. And we are making the distinction between off and on. A nice by-product is that gradually the light stays on longer, but there is no effort behind this sustained awareness."

Duncan reflects for a moment and says, "Gotcha. I still need to remind myself several times a day to pay attention."

He stops and then continues, "You know, the day after you explained all of this to me, I experienced a big shift. It was like someone had just cleaned my windshield. Everything seemed clearer and so much more alive. I find myself longing for more of that. Of course my mind-chatter tries to worry me about that too. Even so, I am noticing there is a shift, subtle and cumulative, that is happening anyway. I've been skiing, and I have been thinking that the visceral excitement of skiing silences the mind. I realized today that awareness of the body, of body sensations, the chill air, the warm boots, this can be pure awareness. It's when meanings and stories start appearing that it's mind-chatter again."

I am surprised at Duncan's insight and the clarity with which he is describing his new level of consciousness. "Let me relate a story to you. What you are describing reminds me of something that Dan Millman described in his book, *The Way of the Peaceful Warrior*. His spiritual teacher, who he calls Socrates, tells him that he thinks too much. Millman is not getting the point so Socrates throws him over a bridge into a small river below. When Millman gets out of the water and climbs back up onto the bridge Socrates says to him, 'you weren't thinking on the way down to the water, where you?'

"The point is that when we are fully engaged in *living* there is no thought, no analysis. That is what you have discovered. It is a wonderful truth. What life presents in each moment is exactly what life is, what it is supposed to be. When the mind goes silent, the silence is immediately filled with life. So we can live in the abundance of eternal life that is unfolding in each moment or we can *think* about it. Doesn't seem like much of a choice."

"Not from my vantage point," affirms Duncan.

I interject, "Before I forget about it, you have said something very important about the practice of Witness Thought Transformation™. You pointed out that you were seeking to regain the feeling that came with the initial breakthrough. Then you indicated that you had a stressful internal dialogue about that. The Practice could not be more easy and simple. It is merely a noticing. Everything that comes after that is the ego-mind looking for an outcome, or measuring its progress, or beating you up for not doing it right. These are very common mind games that people play when they are first learning the Practice."

"Yes, I can see that. I watch my thought and it goes away, and then I tell myself I am not doing it right. I am disappointed with myself, which I know is not productive. My biggest problem is I don't want to screw things up with my work with you, I am so afraid that I'll do something wrong."

"Duncan, that is an ego pattern that has been with you all of your life. In order for you to achieve Mastery, you will have to find the root of that pattern."

I think of Ed and Marissa as I explain this to Duncan. A relationship, like a marriage, is such an incredible crucible for bringing out these patterns. But then again, so is the therapy room.

#

Marissa and Ed's session starts with a question from Marissa. "Okay, is the inner dialogue between itself also random thought or is it me having a dialogue going? Like when I watch my thought and then say to myself something about the thought I just watched."

"For our purposes there actually is no distinction between the two or three. You have identified the inner dialogue, the inner dialogue talking to or about the inner dialogue, and 'me' having a dialogue. It is all the same thing. It is speech without a speaker. It is the ego-mind talking to the ego-mind. But when you make the distinction 'me having a dialogue,' that means you have segmented out certain thoughts that you have identified as *my thoughts*. This is where all of the trouble starts. There are no thoughts that are your thoughts. The ability to maintain an internal dialogue is a *tool*. When you say 'my thoughts,' the tool is now using you.

"So is all verbal thought from the 'monkey'? I am aware that I have an almost constant thought process or dialogue going on. Sometimes it's just decisions I want to make but a lot of the time it's a jumble of scenarios; some ok and some quite destructive. So do even the voices back and forth with each other also come from the monkey?"

"There are two important points that you are raising. First is the question of the monkey. Remember that the Limbic System is required to link up to the prefrontal lobes to create the voice. So the monkey is involved in all verbal thought. The important work for each of us is to distinguish when we get hijacked by it. We know a hijacking has taken place because we have an emotional reaction.

"Now don't get me wrong. If we need to run to save our lives and we feel fear and this causes us to run, then the monkey is doing the job it is supposed to do. On the other hand, if you are running from your husband because you feel uncomfortable being close, then that is a hijacking based on what the monkey learned during those first 5 years of life.

"The monkey was essential when we lived in caves, but in a society it becomes an anachronism."

"I get it," says Marissa. "The monkey is about survival. And the dialogue only gets out of hand when it thinks a situation is about survival."

"Right. Now let's turn to the other thing you said. You have categorized certain dialogues as 'decision making.' What if I told you that the voice in your head is never involved in decision making?"

Marissa looks at me in surprise. "That would definitely be new information."

Ed pipes up, "Honey, great, new information."

Marissa gives him a withering glare and turns to me saying, "Go ahead. I can't take him anywhere."

"Okay, let's take an extremely simple decision that you will be making in this room in a few minutes. You are going to decide to get up off of that couch and leave the room when the session is over. Make sense?"

"Of course."

"I want you to predict what the voice in your head will say to make you stand up from a sitting position."

"Oh, I can answer that. I will just stand up. What a silly idea."

"Precisely. You will just stand up. You will not go inside your head and say to yourself, 'time to stand up.'"

"Of course not. If that were the case I would be going around all day saying 'time to sit,' 'time to eat,' 'time to go to bed.'"

"You are so right. The simple fact is that we do not use verbal thought to make decisions. Remember it is a commentary – after the fact. Decisions are made by the nonverbal part of the brain by taking in information, processing it against the backdrop of the body, in other words the feeling of it, and then we move one way or the other."

Ed leans forward and asks, "What is all this dialogue in my head about decisions then?"

"I am always *processing* before I decide," adds Marissa.

I turn to Marissa and ask, "Tell me, what you mean by *processing*?"

"Well, I mull it over. I talk to myself about the possibilities, I guess."

"Why do you think you do that?"

"I don't know," Marissa reflects. "I guess I don't want to make the wrong decision."

I clap my hands. "Yes! Now tell me what feeling you get while you are doing this?"

She looks at me quizzically, "I don't know."

"Just pretend you have an important decision to make soon. You are in your head discussing it with yourself. As you pretend this, just notice any feeling or sensation you get in your body."

"I feel something right here," she says pointing to her stomach. "It feels like I am anxious!" A surprised look sweeps across her face. "I'm anxious?"

"Yes, so at first it appears that the voice in your head is a decision maker. But in reality what is happening is that you are using self-talk to manage your anxiety. At the moment the decision needs to be made, we just make it. It follows a completely different path."

"You've got to be kidding. All along I thought this dialogue was me deciding. It was really me worrying or creating worries."

"Yep."

Ed says, "Maybe that's what is going on with me. I have been having this issue and some resistance. I notice that I have a hard time sticking to the practice very long. I get this feeling that while I am watching my thoughts, I am not taking care of all the problems I should be working on. I'm burning all this energy talking about Witness Thought Transformation™ and laboring in my head, rather than just letting go and settling into the practice, letting it take its course."

Marissa interjects, "I have to tell you, this voice can be so sneaky," she laughs. "Something happened this morning that in the past would have had me in a panic attack. Because of the food program I am on, which helps me to balance my sugar sensitive biochemistry, I am so much less reactive now. When this thing happened today, I was very emotionally distanced. It would be okay, I was not in trouble. And in being emotionally distanced, I thought I was not thinking about it, nor was I identifying with the thoughts about it. And when I really looked, I was still thinking about it, emotional distance or not. When I realized that, I just stepped back from the thoughts. I found that stepping back from emotion is not the same thing as stepping back from thoughts. This was a good lesson."

Ed says, "I am seeing that my thinking, which now includes the crappy feelings I have much of the time, is arbitrary and judgmental. I am not sure that self preservation is a bad thing, but the *voice* and all these feelings lead to such a poor quality of life that it seems any alternative would be better. I am fatigued and frustrated by the absolute relentlessness of the voice. The more I practice, it seems, the more the voice is there and, although I know the object is not for it to go away, it is so fatiguing to engage it again and again with it saying the same thing again and again and again."

"Can you hear the element of *struggle* and drama in what you are both saying? Witness Thought Transformation™ is not about struggle or drama. It is the simple practice of noticing yourself having a thought. It is an exercise in awareness. You are *engaging* the thoughts, not *noticing* them. Then you are experiencing judgment, struggle and resistance. You are messing with the process of thought."

"Yesterday I had a particularly fatiguing experience with Witness Thought Transformation™," Ed continues as if I had just said nothing. "I was stuck in traffic and decided to use the time and found myself not listening to my thinking but feeling rotten nonetheless. It felt like by not allowing the dialogue of 'woe is me' or 'all these people ahead of me are jerks,' I was escalating the emotional discomfort. Although I had the insight that the feelings go on and even begin without the voice, I could see no relief from the suffering, given that it comes from non-verbal sources I have no contact with!"

"Ed, what you are saying is simply not true. What the voice in your mind says and what you feel are inextricably intertwined. It is just that the verbalization has been repeated so many times for so many years that you no longer notice it. You also seem to be bemoaning the fact that thought watching is taking away from your need to be angry and beat up everyone so you don't get a migraine. My guess is that Marissa has been at the center of this since you have been married. You have to act out your anger so you don't feel even worse. Meanwhile, everyone in the immediate vicinity gets a dose of your toxic waste.

"None of this has anything to do with witnessing thought. Remember, I said to practice on the small thoughts. It seems like you are all caught up in the drama of thought. You're not witnessing, you're messing in your own puddle."

#

Today is Karen's fourth appointment with me. From our previous meetings I took away the feeling that she was not excited about Witness Thought Transformation™. She comes from a violent alcoholic family and she has a very strong set of defenses. All this is a little unsettling since she is the pastor of a local church.

"So, Karen, were you able to integrate any of the practice into your week?"

"Well, I tried but at this time of year in the church there are so many demands on my time. But I did want to get back to why I am depressed. If you will remember, I was a missionary in Peru and I spent most of my tenure there working in the Santa Mónica Prison."

"Right, that must have been terrifying."

"Oh my Lord. There was at least one killing a week there. But I was never afraid. Often times I would get a call in the middle of the night and have to go when the prisoners were rioting. I just remained calm and the guards would let me right in."

"I don't know how you survived."

"But the next thing I knew, after three years of hard, dangerous work, the Plenary Council gives me this assignment here in this suburb. How can I ever prove myself here? I just keep thinking, I must have done something wrong."

"It's all about achievement, isn't it Karen?"

"Doesn't everyone want to achieve something? How am I ever going to amount to anything stuck out in the suburbs like this?"

I can see that Karen is very frustrated with her circumstances. "Where would you rather have gone?"

"I wanted to go to downtown LA. I love the *mean streets*. I want to work in the barrio."

"My god woman, that sounds dangerous again. Have you ever wondered why you are attracted to that sort of environment? Have you ever wondered why you are so depressed over your lack of achievement?"

"I know you say it has to do with my alcoholic family. But I say that is just the way I am."

"Karen, it's a metaphor. Don't you see? Your family was a dangerous place and so you keep going back to the danger. It doesn't matter if it's Peru or the mean streets. It reminds your Limbic System of home."

Karen stares blankly and says, "I know there is probably some influence there. But don't you believe in a *calling*? This is my calling."

"No, what I believe in is a lesson. God is trying to teach you a lesson, but you don't seem to want to learn what God is trying to teach you. You're like a moth drawn to the flame who never questions why she is flying repeatedly, fervently, *and with such passion* back into the flame."

I let that settle for a moment and then I change the subject. "But all of these questions get answered quite easily and obviously if you will just do the thought watching exercise I taught you."

"I just seem to experience a level of discomfort with it. So I watch my thought. Then what am I supposed to do?"

"Karen, just watch your thoughts. That's it. Do only that."

"I am just not comfortable with it, at least not yet. What do you think?"

I chortle. "What do I think? You don't want to know what I think."

Karen looks at me very seriously and says, "No, please, be honest with me."

I draw a deep breath. "Karen, I like you. I thoroughly enjoy our get-togethers. And I respect you. But you are a woman without any psychological insight, with classic defenses from a well-studied type of family background, who claims to be a minister of God. And yet, despite the fact that Paul tells us to 'hold in captivity every thought,' you are not even mildly curious about yours. And yet you have the unmitigated gall to stand in the pulpit every Sunday. What the hell!"

Karen's face goes ashen as I talk. After a long silence she looks at me and says, "Maybe I better start listening. Let's start over. I am ready now."

Chapter 10: The Monkey is Holographic

There is a mechanism in the Limbic System that hijacks us over and over again. As a psychotherapist, I see this in people's lives. They are miserable because of it. Their relationships don't work and are filled with conflict.

The four basic ego or defensive patterns I see on a daily basis involve anger, passive anger, avoidance, and jealousy. These are what we might call *issues, reactive patterns*, or ego patterns. Then there are patterns that are far broader that might be called *life* patterns. A few of these are perfectionism, pleasing, overachieving, projecting strength, and playing the victim.

This chapter deals with a new way of understanding our issues, and how they operate in our lives. No one can ever obtain *mastery* in their life without rising above these patterns. They are the bane of humanity and have kept us in darkness for thousands of years. Awareness is our primary weapon. Awareness takes us to Mastery. Willpower keeps us in slavery.

Inner Speech is Perception

> "Inner speech is to a large extent thinking in pure meanings." (Vygotsky, 1986, p. 249).

Bingo, so there you have it! Perception is meaning making, and in one sentence, Vygotsky ties egocentric speech to perception. But inner speech goes beyond that. Inner speech, egocentric speech, is the organizing principle behind our personal psychology. In chapter 4 we discussed just how the Limbic System processes information. In that section, we made the point that verbal thought is part and parcel of meaning, emotions, motivation and behavior. It turns out that egocentric, inner speech has more influence on our psychology than anyone has even previously suspected. Consider this quote from Vygotsky:

> "The sense of a word, according to [Frederic Paulhan], is the sum of all psychological events aroused in our consciousness by the word. . . . Meaning is only one of the zones of sense, the most stable. A word acquires its sense from the context in which it appears; in different contexts, it changes its sense." (1986, p. 244)

An important aspect of this concept of *sense* would be the emotional packaging of the context. As we have emphasized earlier, emotional context in the brain is regulated by the Limbic System. From a scientific point of view, we might nod wisely and agree that that makes perfect sense (no pun intended). But when you consider the fact that the Limbic System is pretty much wired by 5 years of age give or take, this means that emotional context is learning that takes place very early in life.

What this means is that if my first teenage girlfriend dumps me, this is not some new experience. It will be filtered through whatever learning I might have endured around *rejection* in my formative years. What I actually perceive now is not a neutral, objective representation of what is happening in the *real* world. It is colored by past emotional experiences, which in turn color our current expectations which the Limbic System preconditions. This informs us that substantial distortions will occur to make a perceived event fit those experiences and expectations. Not only that, but via association, perceptions are always formed on the basis of quite limited sensory cues.

Here is where egocentric, inner speech comes home to roost. Researchers have concluded that the structure of language determines the way we perceive the world. What I am stating in the most *emphatic* terms is that the language of a five-year-old dominates how we perceive the world. What does this mean? It means that the brain's language of perceptions comes from a limited vocabulary – that of a five-year-old. For instance, above I used the word "rejection." To a five-year-old that word probably means nothing. How would a child describe *rejection*? "Doesn't care." How would a five-year-old describe *avoidance*? "Get away." How about the concept of *guilt*? "In trouble."

Imagine the Limbic System inside the brain, trapped in the world of a five-year-old. Verbal thought is what connects us to the outside world. But the Monkey has a very limited vocabulary. The list of words and phrases it uses is short and to the emotional point. I call this vocabulary "reactive phrases."

REACTIVE PHRASES ARE HOLOGRAPHIC

So we have the outside world tied to the inside world by linguistics. Our experience of the world is controlled by words and phrases that engage the Limbic System in various survival strategies. Each emotional association activates a neurological *gestalt* that encapsulates the meaning and the experience to which it refers, thereby causing a system wide response or a *reliving* as it were. Freud had something like this in mind when he coined the phrases "ritualistic reenactment" and "repetition compulsion" except this hijacking is on a scale that Freud never dreamed of.

In our heads we have a very short catalog of these words and phrases that serve as beacons that illuminate the patterns that dominate our lives. In chapter 4 we explained the functioning of the Limbic System in terms of *association* and *chaos theory*. To understand how we get hijacked by the ego-mind, we need a more sophisticated metaphor. The hologram is the perfect model for how this hijacking takes place. A hologram is a three dimensional image produced by scattering laser light. We know now that hearing has holographic qualities and more and more scientists are coming to the conclusion that holographic principles mirror how the brain organizes memory and stores information. Consider the diagram below:

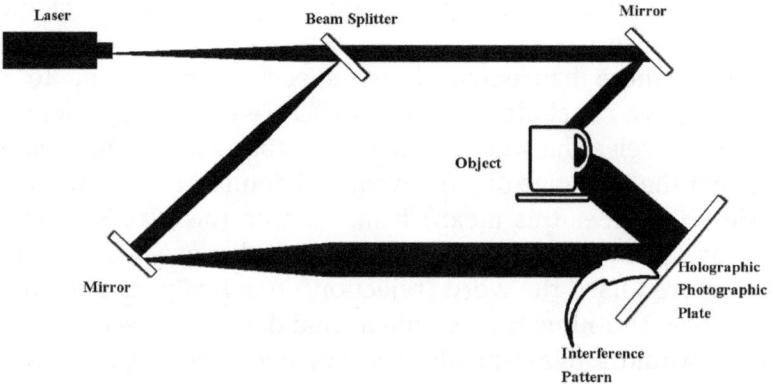

Figure 9: How to create a hologram

The figure shows a simplified diagram of how to create a hologram. First we must use some kind of coherent light. A laser beam is the perfect light for creating holograms. Notice that the beam is split by a beam splitter and then the laser light follows two paths. The light in the first path is shined via a mirror onto the object from which we want to create a hologram, and then onto a photographic, holographic plate. The second is directed via a mirror directly onto the plate. When the two beams converge at the plate an interference pattern is formed thus creating the hologram.

If we look at the plate we don't see the object (cup). We see the interference pattern which looks nothing like the original object. But if we shine a laser through the plate, a three dimensional representation is formed exactly in space where the original object was. We can clearly see the holographic image of the original object.

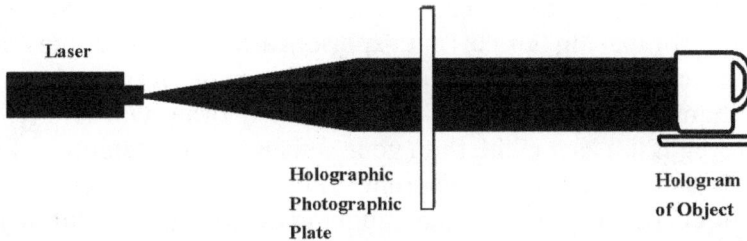

Laser

Holographic
Photographic
Plate

Hologram
of Object

Figure 10: Receating the object

Now let's see if this metaphor helps explain how an issue or reactive pattern gets created and relived over and over. In the next diagram I have tried to substitute the relevant labels to show how this works in the brain.

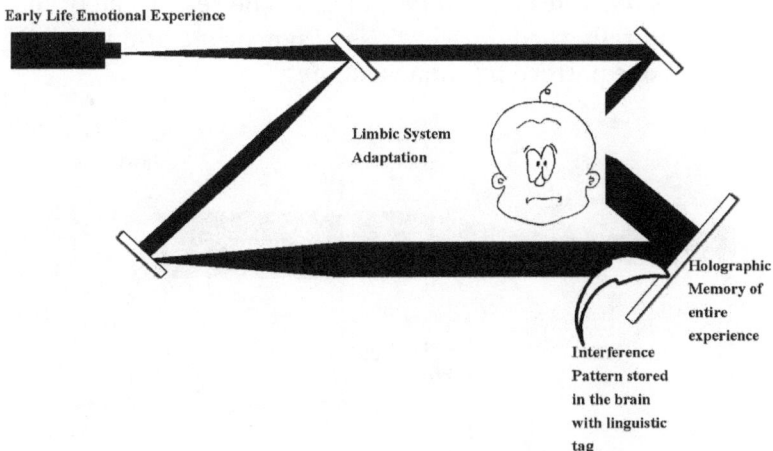

Early Life Emotional Experience

Limbic System
Adaptation

Holographic
Memory of
entire
experience

Interference
Pattern stored
in the brain
with linguistic
tag

Figure 11: Creating a reactive pattern

Emotional experiences early in life and the component reactions to it are encoded like the interference pattern of a hologram. The experience itself is like a laser beam that collides with the perception, feelings and adaptive behaviors creating this ego-pattern or reactive pattern. This then becomes a holographic memory stored in the brain in a similar fashion to the hologram stored on the photographic plate.

The many emotional experiences that happen to us in those first five years create a short catalog of *reactive phrases* that tag the sum total of the entire experience around the reactive pattern. Remember, for the child and the child's monkey brain, this is all about *survival* so the stakes are high. Encoded in the holographic pattern that is formed are meaning, perception, feeling, behavior, and motive along with the visual images that are associated with the origin of that category of experience.

Now years later the survival scanners in the Limbic System are sorting and comparing our current experience. Make no mistake about it, this is a preconditioning. I liken it to the old saying, "if the only tool you have is a hammer, everything looks like a nail." In other words, if *rejection* was your big issue as a child, then your senses will be heightened to the possibility of rejection in your current experience.

If our current experience gets caught in the fuzziness of the attractor pattern for that issue, a *reactive phrase* goes off in the head and the gestalt of the entire experience floods the central nervous system and the body. We then re-experience the original event as if it is the experience we are currently having. This is what I call a *hijacking*. We might say we are having a *holographic* rather than a *real* experience. This represents a global change in the brain's state. Obviously it is initiated by the Limbic System, but its tentacles extend into most of the rest of the brain. Before you know it, literally, the entire brain is in synchronization with this *issue* and the defensive pattern has hijacked Life.

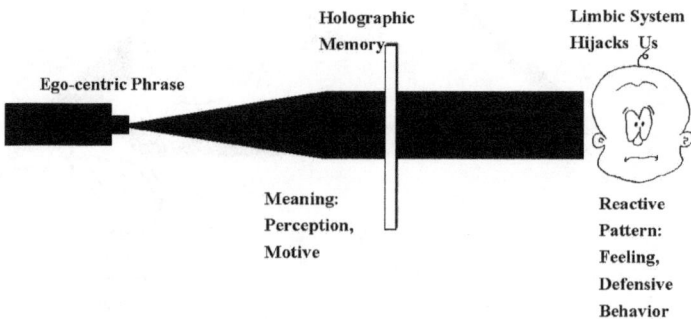

Figure 12: Hijacking our current experience

74

Now I must admit that while the holographic model of brain/body states probably fails in many ways in its elegance and accuracy, I believe it gives us a reasonable way of understanding how the monkey tends to run our lives. The important point here is that egocentric (inner) speech is almost like a binder that ties all of the elements of this pattern together. Then later in life, this *reactive phrase* illuminates and fires off the pattern. But just like the laser that illuminates the hologram, the pattern emerges whole, instantaneously, and we find ourselves in the world of that five-year-old *while believing we are in the world of the adult.*

DISSECTING REACTIVE PHRASES

In the first part of this book, egocentric or inner speech was presented as if it sounds just like normal, social speech. Even in our heads we tend to talk in complete sentences. A sentence, if we remember from grammar school, contains a subject and a predicate. The subject is the *doer* of the sentence and the predicate does the *work* of the sentence. If you notice your everyday inner dialogue as you must do when you are practicing Witness Thought Transformation™, you notice that our rehearsal, regurgitation, and recapitulation is in complete sentences.

This is not the case with *reactive phrases*. Vygotsky found that inner speech became more and more biased toward the predicate part of speech in the children he researched. There is a new syntax that gradually takes hold, and the child starts boiling down inner speech, condensing it as times goes on. Ultimately only the predicate is left. This makes total sense when you contrast this against what we said about the amygdala and the limbic structures involved with speech. Limbic speech is more guttural, so we would expect that articulation would give way to specialization. In other words, reactive phrases become truncated and take on the characteristics of limbic grunting since all we need is the associative trigger to match a pattern. When it comes to survival, talk is cheap!

What we have here are two distinctive types of inner speech in our adult heads. The first are complete sentences and dialogues that have a well formed lexicon. The second are these *reactive phrases* that have been truncated in one way or another. That is why I use the word "phrase," since these hot button words are often not complete sentences. It goes without saying that since the Limbic System is fully developed so early that these phrases and word combinations exhibit the simplicity of a child.

I don't mean to infer that it is *baby talk*. These reactive phrases are short, punchy, and powerful, but they are also simple, declarative statements that use the limited vocabulary of a child and, at the same time, tap into vocalizations that produce meaning in the Limbic System.

For example, earlier we used the word "rejection." A *reactive phrase* would probably never use that word. The phrase "don't care" is far more likely. Also, based on Vygotsky's research, it is likely that the phrase would not be a complete sentence such as, "They don't care about me." Rather it would be more on the order of "don't care." Reactive phrases are inner speech as guttural as they are verbal.

Reactive phrases are biased toward the *sense* of the word rather than its *meaning*. As we stated earlier, the *sense* of a word contains the sum total of the psychological events that are attached to it. Since the Limbic System is wired up when we are so young, it is more than likely that the psychological sense of a reactive phrase is tied to early childhood memories. My work with people confirms this.

In summary, a reactive phrase is a short *punchy* set of words that carries huge emotional impact. It is the organizing principle behind an *issue*, and the entire issue can be recreated by association with whatever personal interaction activates the phrase. We will see examples of this shortly.

MEMORY

When we get caught in a defensive pattern, the state, strategy, and meaning are loaded into the brain and central nervous system in a fraction of a second. This is a hijacking of immense proportions. We are certainly aware of the perception that accompanies it. We are not aware of the distortion to our perception since we think our interpretation is right on target. The feelings that we have are often hard to ignore, although I must say that many people have no real awareness of their feelings. They are so used to simply acting out the pattern that they fail to look deeper than the surface. Blaming, rationalization, and justification are far easier than self-reflection. The defensive behavior that manifests as part of the pattern is easy to spot. These behaviors fall neatly into those that mimic fight or flight.

The one dimension of the pattern that is never in our awareness is the interwoven memories that are the packaging of the pattern. Fortunately, the *reactive phrase* is the key to recovering the memories. This requires a bit of clarification. Ego-patterns don't come from trauma necessarily. It is quite common for people to assume that the issue stems from being mistreated on one occasion or another. Nothing could be farther from the truth.

The parental behavior that encourages the formation of defensive patterns is sustained over time. For instance, constant unfavorable comparison to a sibling, a pattern of criticism and shaming, or parenting that is coercive or intrusive fall more into what would be called *characteristics* of the family rather than *events*. Nonetheless, these treatment sets form a cohesive memory of the *sense* of what it was like to be raised by mom or dad.

The point here is that the specific memory of why one has a particular defensive pattern may remain hidden. Even if it does not, the moment to moment impact of it certainly does. In other words, I may have an intellectual memory of having sustained a lot of criticism as a child, but tying that to the argument I am currently having with my wife can seem preposterous.

It is essential to see the pattern along with the memories associated with it in order to be set free and achieve some kind of Mastery. The revelation of this comes as a "aha" type of experience that often will set a person free from the pattern in the moment of illumination.

The key to accessing the memories along with the holographic image of the entire pattern is the *reactive phrase*. From a therapeutic standpoint, recovering the reactive phrase is relatively simple, albeit a little counterintuitive. The good news is that we all have an advantage when it comes to setting ourselves free. I have discovered a truth that makes this phase of the process relatively easy. You see, the monkey can easily be fooled!

CHAPTER 11: TRICKING THE MONKEY

Duncan sits in the chair beaming as he looks at me. "I get it, Doc. Oh my gosh, do I get it. I have never felt this way before. It is like having a new lease on life."

"Welcome to the real world. But I hope you realize the work is not over."

Duncan looks a little stunned and asks, "What do you mean? Nothing can ever take away the feeling I have right now."

I chuckle and say, "I hate to break the news to you, but that feeling will subside. It becomes routine after a while and fades. Also, the stress of life will make it come and go."

"Bummer!" snorts Duncan, "You could have gone all day without telling me that."

I lean forward. "Duncan, the important thing to realize is that the *knowing* that comes with this level of consciousness will never leave. But there are some dangers and challenges ahead, and I want to prepare you for them."

"Okay, I'm ready."

"This new level of awareness can easily be co-opted by the ego unless you stay vigilant. The ego will convince you that you *know*, that you got it, and before you know it you will be back into the drama. I see many people who have the breakthrough that you have had who turn and walk back into the fire – back into the drama."

"Dear Lord, don't let me do that," states Duncan.

I say, "I am going to do everything in my power to prevent that from happening. That is why we need to move to Mastery."

"Mastery, what's that?"

"Mastery is when you not only move to a higher level of awareness and you are no longer *thought* identified, but you also *overcome* your ego patterns."

"My ego patterns?"

"Another way of labeling them might be to call them *reactive patterns* or *defensive patterns*. These are the emotions and behaviors that are a sure sign that we have been hijacked by the monkey."

"Oh, you mean when I get defensive."

"What most people think of when they say defensive is anger. But let me ask you, what do you do when your wife gets angry?"

Duncan's entire face and body suddenly change. Remembering his wife's anger has obviously resulted in a state change for him. "I just want to run. I want to get away."

"Duncan, are you noticing that it is as if she is here right now getting ready to go out of control? Can you see what happened to you when I mentioned your wife's anger?"

"Doc, don't get me wrong. I love her. She is not all that angry. It's just that . . ."

"Duncan, notice your body right now. What feeling are you having?"

"Oh, my God, I am anxious," he looks at me in surprise.

"Now take a deep breath." I wait for him to settle down a little. "Can we look at what just happened?"

"Please, it's the damndest thing." Duncan takes another breath. "What the heck just happened?"

"The monkey got tricked!"

"What? The monkey got tricked?"

"Think about it for a second. All I did was mention your wife getting angry, and you went into something close to a full panic."

"I guess I did. I never looked at it before like that. What is going on with me?"

"Okay, your wife is not here. It is just you and me. But the mere mention of her anger sent you into a state. We know that emotional reactions come from the Limbic System. Somehow the monkey must have taken what I said and associated it with something within you. Boom, there you were in a full panic. What I am saying is that the monkey got tricked."

The room is silent for a few minutes as Duncan takes this in. Then a look of complete surprise comes over his face. "The monkey doesn't know my wife. It's a five-year-old. What the hell is going on?"

Now it's my turn to be stunned. Duncan has just connected the dots in a big way. "Right, the Limbic System just thinks that your wife is the *person*, the *relationship*. So obviously this goes deep doesn't it?"

"You mean this relates somehow to my parents?"

"Let's find out. What do you think?"

"Yes, let's go for it."

"Okay, so you know how to watch your thoughts, right?"

"Right."

"What I want you to do is merely witness what the voice in your head says. Meanwhile, I am going to trigger the pattern, *fool the monkey*. As the pattern is activated, try to notice what the voice says."

"Okay."

"Now, we are not trying to relive any feelings. Those may come up, but catharsis is not the objective here at all. As a matter of fact, catharsis is often a misguided use of therapy. So my goal is insight, not to have you re-experience every bad thing that ever happened to you."

"That's a relief."

"Okay, here comes your wife and she's angry. What comes up inside?"

Duncan sits quietly waiting. "Nothing, I don't hear the voice saying anything."

"When I said your wife was angry, did you get a hit of anxiety?"

"Oh yeah!"

"Okay, so we tricked the monkey. Just be patient. This takes some time and it seems like it is a little counterintuitive. So here comes your wife and she's angry. What does the voice in your head say?"

"I gotta get away?"

"You're guessing. Don't guess and don't analyze. Just watch. Your wife is coming and she's angry."

"I can feel the anxiety as soon as you say that."

"What we are looking for is a phrase like a five-year-old would say. Not baby talk, but a very simple uncomplicated statement that goes along with the anxiety and the need to flee."

"Okay, try again."

"Here she comes and she's angry."

"I always used to feel this way when I was young. My mother would come screaming at me."

"Why would your mother come screaming at you?"

"Well, she would only do that when I was in trouble." He laughs and then suddenly stops with a stricken look on his face.

"That's it isn't it? The voice in your head says, 'I'm in trouble.'"

"Oh, my god! This is sick! The monkey thinks my wife is my mother."

"Yes, all these years, every time your wife got angry (and probably many times when she didn't get angry she only seemed angry or you assumed she was angry) you got hijacked by your Limbic System into thinking that you were in trouble with your mother."

"Wow that was powerful." Duncan shakes his head back and forth as he contemplates what just happened. I let the energy in the room settle a little.

Finally he looks up at me and asks, "And this is Mastery? I mean, don't get me wrong. This is huge. But . . ."

"Mastery comes from being able to ID this pattern as soon as it comes up. We know all of the pieces of the pattern now. You think you're in trouble, you feel anxious, and you want to escape. But the organizing object in the mind that causes the entire pattern to unfold is the egocentric phrase 'I'm in trouble.'"

"Okay, so as soon as I think of my wife coming in the room or calling me, I am saying to myself 'uh oh' or 'in trouble' and then I react as if I am in trouble."

"Yes, now the way to Mastery is to study this reaction until you master it as it arises inside of you. Sometimes you might only notice the avoidance or the escaping. It might also take the form of making excuses or explaining. Sometimes you might actually feel the anxiety. Then again there will be times when you hear the triggering phrase from your inner voice. Each time that happens, sit down and try to put all the pieces together and realize that this is a hijacking and it is all about mom."

"Wow, sounds like a lot of work."

"Think of it as digging a tunnel out of prison. It is surely a lot of work, but freedom is the reward.

"Now let me ask you something. How do you think life has been for your wife living with you?"

"I don't know. What do you mean?"

"Think about it. Many times when she interacts with you, you act like you're 'in trouble.' Imagine what it is like for her to be with someone who is always in trouble, who is always defensive because he thinks he has done something wrong."

"She probably feels as if she is a critical parent," Duncan replies. "She probably feels like she is a truant officer instead of in a loving relationship. Man, I have really screwed up. Damn my monkey."

"Duncan, you haven't screwed up. You have awakened. Don't you see that dealing with you is bringing up something inside of her that she needs to see? It becomes clear that the purpose of your relationship is to make you conscious not happy. The entire universe has aligned itself to help you see this 'I'm in trouble' pattern and set you free from it so you can have a happy relationship with your wife."

#

I find myself wondering if Ed and Marissa have finally experienced the breakthrough that comes with Witness Thought Transformation™. When I last saw them it seemed that they were taking the practice and creating drama out of it. There is a point of surrender when the person just gives in to the simplicity of the practice without resistance and endless analysis.

Ed sits down and leans forward like he is ready to go. "Okay, you win. After I left here the last time, I realized that I was doing just about everything but what you wanted me to do."

I chuckle and motion for him to continue. He takes a deep breath and says, "My breakthrough came when I was shaving the other day. I was standing there in front of the mirror and I heard myself say, 'I don't need to watch my thoughts. Waller doesn't know what he is talking about.' You know, I suddenly became aware I was experiencing a thought. It was my voice talking to me, but it was like it wasn't me anymore. It was just this voice with this extremely hostile, arrogant tone. As soon as I had this awareness, it stopped. It was in *that* moment that I think I got it. That is all I was supposed to do, right?"

"That's it. You just became aware that thinking was happening in the moment it was happening."

"Okay, I just kept doing that. I would just notice the voice and it would stop. The next thing I notice, my stress was gone. It took only a few minutes and boom, my stress was gone. It's all about thought, isn't it? I just hope Marissa has the same experience I had. I feel free."

Marissa smiles and says, "Oh, I had the same breakthrough that Ed did. He has just been so excited, I didn't want to ruin his fun."

"Tell me, how did you experience your breakthrough?" I ask Marissa.

"Well, when I left last time, I was thinking about drama. I wondered to myself, 'why do I need this endless rehearsal in my head?' So I decided to watch the rehearsal. Of course, just as you say, I found that I couldn't watch it. It would start, I would notice, it would stop. I found that I started to feel better, like more relaxed. I think I really did feel a shift of some kind, but it took a little longer than Ed's."

"That's great. I am so happy for both of you."

Marissa says, "Then it was as if something happened to our relationship. We have been like two lovebirds all week."

"It is, just as you said, a lot like getting a new set of eyes," says Ed. "But I have a question?"

"What's that, Ed?"

"Why am I so damn angry? After this breakthrough, I really felt like I was in 'the peace that passes all understanding.' But that lasted for about two days. Then I was right back griping at traffic and struggling with this angry dialogue in my head. What gives? I thought all of that would go away."

"Welcome to the human condition," I reply with a note of irony. "Now you must become the master over those patterns that have hounded you all of your life."

"Oh, man! How can I do that? There are so many of them."

"Actually the good news is that for you there are probably only two of them you really need to be concerned about. In fact, when you get angry there is only one pattern. It just keeps reappearing in various forms in every area of your life."

"How can I get after it? I mean what do I need to do to get it to stop?"

"Ah, that's the trick. We are not going to get it to stop. We are going to shine the light on it. Think of it this way. Let's say you have been blindsided by a curve ball all of your life. If you could clearly see it coming at you, what would you do?"

"I guess I would duck."

"Yes, you would get out of the way. This would be far more effective than standing there shouting at Life not to throw any more curve balls. So that's what we will do, give you the kind of sight you need to see the pattern around anger so that you can duck!"

"Makes sense except how am I going to do that? You keep talking about a hijacking. That's what it feels like, but I don't notice it until the plane is going down in flames."

I turn to Marissa and ask, "Do you mind if we use you as an example?"

"Glad to help, just don't get mad at me, Ed."

"Thanks. Okay here is what we are going to do. We are going to trick Ed's monkey."

Ed turns to Marissa and says, "Then we can spank . . ."

"Wrong monkey, big boy." Marissa cuts him off. "Just pay attention to the doctor."

I decide to ignore the entire interaction and go on to the exercise. "Ed, what does she do that gets you the most upset?"

"Oh, that's easy. She ignores me."

I immediately hold up my hand to Marissa. "Now don't defend. This is an exercise, Marissa. What I want you to do is to ignore him. No matter what he says to you, I don't want you to answer back. Okay?"

"Yep, you got it."

"Okay, Ed. I want you to say something to Marissa, but when you do, I want you to simply witness the voice in your head."

"I'm not supposed to react?"

"Allow the reaction to happen, but notice what the voice in your head says as the reaction happens."

Ed gets quiet and I initiate the pattern. "Ok, Ed, ask Marissa if she wants to have lunch after the session today."

He turns to her and asks, "Would you like to get lunch after we leave?"

She remains silent and I notice there is more color in Ed's cheeks.

"Are you feeling angry?"

"Yes."

"What does the voice in your head say?"

"Something like 'screw her.'"

"Okay, so slow the whole process down and just be watchful. You know we are tricking the monkey and you will feel anger. But we are looking for a key phrase that unlocks the meaning of the whole experience. Ask her again."

"Want to have lunch?" We wait in silence and Ed says, "She doesn't care about me."

"I think 'doesn't care' is a pretty good answer, but let's look further. When you were a little boy, who would ignore you?"

"Nobody ignored me that I can remember."

"Just think back. Were either of your parents not around?"

"My dad never came to my baseball games even though I was *All State*. He just didn't care. He always treated me like I didn't matter."

I have done a lot of this work and when I hear the egocentric phrase that is at the root of a pattern, it always resonates with me. The phrase 'didn't matter' has that kind of ring to it. I wonder if Ed has picked up on it too.

Ed looks at me and then looks at Marissa. I can see a tear forming in the corner of his eye. Tears gush out of both eyes and he reaches for a tissue. "I don't matter. I don't matter," he sobs.

Marissa puts her hand on the back of his neck and gently rubs.

"That's the phrase isn't it? 'You don't matter.' When Marissa ignores you, you don't matter. When someone cuts you off on the freeway, you don't matter. It's all about that isn't it?"

Ed takes a few minutes to regain his composure wiping his eyes and blowing his nose. "Dear Lord, what just happened? It was as if Marissa, the entire world, had become my father who treated me like I didn't matter."

"In essence, that is exactly what happened. Your Limbic System thinks you live in a world, the world of your father, where you don't matter. It applies that template to everything when it can sweep your experience into that associative bucket. It is a system-wide hijacking and you just saw it for the first time."

"But why now? I have looked at this before and couldn't see it. Why this time?"

"It's that particular phrase, 'don't matter.' When you said 'doesn't care' nothing happened. Somehow in the child's mind the *don't matter* phrase encapsulated all of the pain. The *doesn't care* phrase was probably equally true but it did not encode all of the meaning and pain in the Limbic System. Getting the exact phrase is the key to unlocking the true identity of the hijacker, of seeing the entire pattern for what it is."

Chapter 12: The Reactive Phrase

You can see in the previous examples that when the right combination of words is found the entire reactive pattern reveals itself. I agree with Vygotsky that there needn't be a subject, that the predicate is what packs the emotional punch. From the standpoint of the brain, it is as if the Limbic System has taken speech and boiled it down to a guttural vocalization that allows it to be the key to an entire holographic process. When the exact phrase is revealed, not only is the pattern revealed, but the truth of the pattern's origin is also revealed. The impact of this on the individual is profound. They do the see that the trigger for the pattern has been manufactured and that the genesis of the pattern is far back in time and related to a person who is no longer part of present life experience.

Even if the parent to which the pattern is associated is still alive, the person experiences that parent in a totally different frame of reference than that encapsulated by the pattern. This is very much an experience in time traveling. The person is immediately catapulted back to the days when the original pain was formed. They see very clearly how it is all interrelated. But most profound of all, they see how ridiculous and out of place the reactive pattern is in their everyday life. This is not to say that they cannot clearly see how the pattern is being associated. Of course they see the tone of voice, body language, verbalizations, all of which causes the Limbic System to sweep them into the pattern. But the one thing that stands out when this reliving occurs, whether with the help of a therapist or not, is the total absurdity of it. It is quite normal while a person is re-experiencing the original woundedness from which the pattern emerged for them to laugh through their tears!

This unleashes a tremendous insight that this pattern that has dogged them all of their lives is ridiculous, outlandish, and has no place in their current world. The sense of being hijacked is overwhelming. The absurdity of it produces surprise, laughter, shock, tears and, often times, utter disbelief that such a thing is even happening.

THINKING IN PURE MEANINGS

At this point I would like to emphasize the distinction between verbal thought and what I am calling a *reactive phrase*. We experience verbal thought on two different levels. At the highest level it is just the constant rehearsal, regurgitation, and speculation of that egocentric voice that sounds like you talking to you. If I am thinking of what I will say to my wife, I am thinking in full sentences as if I was saying it out loud. If I am writing, I am subvocalizing entire sentences. If I am reading I am doing the same thing in my head.

Reactive phrases are an entirely different animal. We might call them thinking in pure meanings. The phrase itself is the verbal tip of the proverbial iceberg; underneath is a system-wide response that includes cognitions, behavior, emotions, memory and expectations. These are inextricably linked. We might say that from a nonverbal point of view, the pattern is a thought, no part of which is able to be separated from the whole.

This is why traditional therapy has such a hard time breaking through these patterns. Cognitive behavioral therapy goes after the hot thought. Insight-oriented therapy espouses an understanding of patterns from a psychodynamic point of view. Other approaches recommend working through the feelings. But just like a holographic plate, if you break it into pieces, the whole is still embedded in each piece.

Uncovering the *reactive phrase* illuminates the entire thought system at once holistically. It is like being able to see the big picture, the 900 pound gorilla in the room – pick your favorite metaphor. The net effect of this is the uncovering of the hijacker. The experience of this shifts from me and my issues to "what the hell is that doing in me."

The reactive phrase is the binder between the Limbic System and the outside world. The belief that the voice in our heads is who we are gives the reactive phrase the cover it needs to operate unencumbered for the rest of our lives. The practice of Witness Thought Transformation™ frees us from the illusion that the voice in our heads is "me" and confirms the belief that whatever is going on in my head is "not me."

Therefore the combination of achieving witness consciousness and no longer being thought identified is a huge asset when it comes to tracking down the patterns that keep sabatoging our lives.

The Path to Mastery

There is a path of mastery that leads one to break the bonds of limbic slavery. In my experience it is enormously helpful to experience the reactive phrase in order to break the code of the pattern, but it is not absolutely necessary in achieving Mastery in one's life. What is necessary in any event is to realize fully that a reaction is a pointer that highlights to what is unhealed. It points to the burden we have carried since childhood. And it points to the stress of a parental relationship that did not go as we might have wanted. But even more vital is that it points to unconsciousness.

When we become ensnared in a reactive pattern we go unconscious. Our objective should be *conscious living*. This does not mean we never react. What it does mean is that we eventually learn so well the tricks of the ego mind that we clearly see the pattern as soon as it appears and that we can, *in real time,* make adjustments before or as the hijacking begins to take us over.

This is where relationships are so valuable in moving us toward mastery. What keeps coming up in relationships is the very thing we need to look at to set ourselves free. The purpose of a relationship is to make us conscious, not happy. This is a bitter pill to many of us. But if you think about it, it makes perfect sense. How could a relationship actually be happy if it is not conscious?

Life is a mirror reflecting back the effects of mind patterns. The Buddha said, "With our thoughts we create our world." So the world points back to us, at what is inside of us. Each time a reactive pattern fires, it is an opportunity to look inside and go deeper. Witness Thought Transformation™ is the light we need to look inside. Through witnessing thought, we know that thought, voices, and patterns are objects in consciousness that can be inspected.

So every time the pattern gets activated, we stop and ask, "What just happened?" "How does this relate to mom or dad?" "What am I feeling right now?" "What is my perception of what just happened?" The final critical question to ask is, "What did the voice in my head just say?"

At first it is hard to realize we have been hijacked. We might not even realize it until the next day. But with dedication we can narrow that time gap until there is a moment of true self-observation when we witness the gnarly thing rising up inside of us in real time. This leads to liberation. It is an awareness, a remembering of who we really are. We are not thought. We are not mind patterns. We are the Awareness that's watching.

Presence

We hear a lot about *presence*, being in the *now*, mindfulness and so forth. For many this seems like a mystery. The reason it is such a conundrum is that you cannot use the mind to find Presence. Awareness is like the flipside of Presence. When we are aware we are present with our current experience.

We are often guided by enlightened or awakened teachers to be present with a flower or with the vista of a country-side or whatever. We are told to just become aware of the flower. If this leaves you a little cold, you are not alone. How are we to enter into Presence?

Practitioners of Witness Thought Transformation™ have an advantage. They have instant access to Presence by virtue of witnessing thought. How can that be? When Awareness watches, thoughts stop, and what's left is Presence. Not to turn this into a word game, but Awareness is Presence. So the more we are aware of thought, the more we become aware of the absence of thought. When mental activity is silenced, the Presence of Awareness is experienced as the stillness that is watching.

Eventually when one practices thought watching, and looks at thoughts deeply, there is an awareness that there is no *watcher* and the experience transforms into the Unity of being which the sages have called *Enlightenment*.

CHAPTER 13: THE MONKEY SETS YOUR HAIR ON FIRE

I watch expectantly as Lisa walks into the room and sits down. There is certainly something different about her air, her carriage – something.

"Okay," she begins, "Forget about all that stuff we talked about before."

"I thought the things we talked about were very important."

"They were. They are." She seems almost breathless. "But I don't want to talk about that right now. I want to tell you about my week. And I want to know if I am doing it right."

"Doing what right?" I ask.

"You know, witness thought transfusion or whatever you call it."

"Witness Thought Transformation™. You tried it?"

Lisa almost gulps for air. "Tried it. Tried it! It changed my life. Of course I tried it. You told me to, didn't you?"

"Yes. What happened?"

Lisa sits back. "Well, I did what you told me to do. You know how I was when I was here last time, my mind constantly saying, 'I'm a piece of shit; I'm a piece of shit.' Well it suddenly dawned on me that I was in my head saying, 'I'm a piece of . . .' What I mean is that I saw myself saying it to myself."

"You stepped back."

"Yes, that's a good way of saying it. It felt like being in another space or room or something. But I saw myself repeating these words over an over. Then I realized, that's what you were asking me to do, just to notice that I am thinking."

I lean forward. "And?"

"So I did. Each time I had a thought about my nails, my shoes, my clothes -- my gosh, I sound like I am a slave to fashion!-- I just started to notice the voice in my head. Then it struck me."

"What? You had some realization?"

"Yes, there are no *problems* unless you *think*. What I mean is that without a thought, there is no history of abuse, there is no self-hatred. There is only this." With that Lisa shrugs and gestures to the emptiness of the room.

Lisa seems pleased with herself, but it is nothing to the pleasure of what I am experiencing. It is like watching the birth of a new life right here in front of me.

"Do you get what I am saying? Right here right now, there is no abuse. A memory is just a thought, and when I try to inspect the thought, the thought disappears. It keeps happening. And every time it does, I go free. I feel new every time I do it."

"Actually, truth be known, you are new."

"I know, I know. I can be free. I can also see that it is a choice. I have to make this choice for freedom in every moment. But I have to say, it took a few hours for the realization to finally set in."

I laugh, "Only a few hours?"

"Well, I would start talking to myself, and then I would realize that my self-talk was going. The instant I realized it, it would stop. Then there was this moment when I asked myself, 'if I am not that voice, then what am I?'

"I don't know quite yet, but I am gonna find out come hell or high water. Can you imagine, all those years of suffering going away so quickly? But I know one thing for certain."

"What's that?" I ask.

"When I watch the voice in my head, the instant it goes silent I know that I am not that abused little girl. I don't know what or who I really am, but I know I am not that girl. There is no more identification with it at all. I am free of her."

"Yes, but what about all of that pain?"

"Oh, the pain is still there. Every now and then I can feel the pain. And you know what is weird? I can remember it all now. But it is like I am outside of the box. It is all over there." She point to the corner of the room. "And I am over here. So, yes, the pain is still there and it invites me into it. But as long as I watch my thoughts, I don't go there."

I clear my voice. "I can't tell you how happy I am."

Lisa looks at me. "Thank you so much. All I had to do was what you told me. It was so simple and so fast, I can't believe it. It's like I am not dragging this burden around with me anymore. And all I had to do was just catch myself thinking and within a short period of time the spell was broken!"

"Well, I guess my work here is done."

"Not so fast, Doc. I don't know how to trust this new awareness yet. I am going to stick to you like glue until I am surer of myself."

"I can't think of anyone I would be more honored to have stuck to me!"

We both laugh and I know that Lisa has taken a huge step into a much bigger world.

#

Duncan takes his seat in front of me looking like the cat that ate the canary. "Oh, my God! Oh, my God. That's all I can say. I think I am in trouble all the time. Dear Lord."

I chuckle and inquire for more details.

"I mean this thing we discovered last time, this 'I'm in trouble' pattern. I can see that it has literally invaded my entire life. The phone rings and there it is. My wife says, 'good morning' and there it is. This, what you call a 'reactive pattern,' must get triggered about one hundred times a day. My gut is churning, my mind is going. It's like I am running a thousand miles an hour with my hair on fire. Good grief."

"It's pervasive."

"Pervasive? Hell, it's oozing out of my pores. My God, I spend most of my day with my eyes rolled back in my head!"

"Wow, it sounds as if you have had a tremendous insight."

"Oh, and that's only half of it. Every time I feel the fear of being in trouble, I just switch the emotional switch to off and act as if there is nobody home inside. Talk about a level of protection. I can't believe I have lived like this all these years."

"It is pretty scary when you consider that this is how all of humanity spends most of their time."

Duncan leans forward in his chair. "It's insanity I tell you. And you know what's even worse?"

I shrug my shoulders.

"I can see how insane everyone else is! They are all inside listening to the voice in their head just automatically doing whatever it says."

"It sounds like you have had an interesting week," I laugh.

Duncan gets serious for a moment. "I talked with my wife about this. We decided that we would work together. Every time she notices me shutting down or every time I notice myself feeling nervous, we are going to talk about it. I think I have made more progress toward what you call mastery in one week than in my previous life. My reactive pattern is all we have been talking about. By the way, she says she is going to call you. She wants to see what is going on with her."

"Wow, that's great. You know this opens up the opportunity for something wonderful."

"What's that?" asks Duncan.

"A conscious relationship," I reply.

"Lately, it is as if we were just married. There is a closeness and a level of communication we haven't had for years. I want more! Oh, and at work, I am more confident. I spend more time pumping out the work and less time stewing in my own juices.

"I swear to you, I will never stop watching my thoughts and studying these patterns. I never want to feel like that again. Getting caught in my ego mind is like swimming in a septic tank. Every time I go back into the pattern, I feel like I need a shower."

I laugh at the allusion to the septic tank. That really is very close to what it feels like to go back to being unconscious once one has tasted Presence.

"Duncan, I really appreciate hearing that level of commitment to your Awakening. Is there another pattern that you have been struggling with?"

Duncan goes quite for a moment and finally looks at me surprised. "Jealously, is that a pattern?"

"Of course."

"Well then I have it. The feeling is overpowering. I'm not sure I can even define the feeling. But when it gets a hold on me, I am lost and overwhelmed."

"Well, let's take a look."

"Okay. . ." Duncan agrees with some fear and trepidation in his voice.

"Tell me what circumstance brings up the jealousy more than any other."

Duncan thinks for a moment and then says, "When my wife goes to the store without me. That would be a good example. After about fifteen minutes I have overwhelming feeling that she is cheating on me."

"Ok, perfect. So I want you to imagine that your wife has gone to the store and it has been some time now. What does the voice in your head say?"

"She better get home? She is with someone else?"

"Duncan, you're guessing. You know how to watch your thoughts, right?"

He nods.

"So what I want you to do is just be the watcher. There is nothing to figure out. Just slow the entire process down and look."

I begin again, "Okay, your wife has been gone for quite a while. What does the voice say?"

"That she is meeting someone else. No, wait that's just me talking again. Do it again."

"You wife should have been home by now. What does the voice in your head say?"

Duncan looks at me questioningly. "I don't know what it says. It just seems like she prefers someone else better than me. But who is that other person?"

"Forget that for right now. Remember, we are looking for a phrase that a five-year-old might say. A five-year-old would never use the term 'jealousy.' That's too big a word. So we are looking for a key phrase that is simple and declarative that encompasses the meaning of what is happening."

"You know, when you said 'five-year-old' I had a flash of something. When I was young my older brother got to go everywhere with my Dad. I always got stuck home with my mother. It was pretty obvious that he was Dad's favorite. I guess he just liked him better."

"Duncan, I think we are on to something very big here. Your wife has been gone a long time. What does the voice say?"

"Oh, my god! She likes him better. The voice is saying 'likes him better!' Can it be that simple?"

I laugh. "Meet the Limbic System. That is exactly what is happening. When she leaves and is gone for a certain period of time, the voice in your head says, 'likes him better' and you are flooded with jealousy. The monkey thinks that your wife has gone off with another man, just as your father would leave with your brother."

"You have got to be kidding. This is ridiculous. My poor wife! I am always so sure that she is cheating. And yet I know she isn't. No wonder . . . my father . . . my brother . . ."

"Duncan, what I have found is that the root of jealousy is always some form of comparison that we make early in life. This is usually encouraged by biased and poisoned parenting."

"I never thought of my father as a bad parent."

"It is not all that unusual for a parent to pick a favorite and constantly rub that in the face of the least-favored child. This can be devastating. It results in a special form of insecurity that involves a comparison. This torments us for the rest of our lives. The monkey brain is constantly trying to right the wrong and restore balance into our relationships."

"He did say all kinds of cruel things about me at the same time as he would praise my brother. You know what's funny? To this day, Dad is still doing that and ironically my brother can't hold a job and is an alcoholic. Go figure."

"That just goes to show you how misplaced the jealousy is. It also tells you that it must be coming from the Limbic System through an associative, reactive pattern since nothing in your current world validates the belief that someone is better than you in the eyes of your wife or anyone else."

"The voice in my head?"

"So now every time you start having this experience, just stop and ask yourself what this has to do with Dad and the whole pattern of emotional rivalry will reveal itself."

"You said rivalry. Is this what they call sibling rivalry?"

"I believe jealousy is deeper than that. Also, I have had clients who were *onlys* so there was no rival who was a sibling."

#

Ed and Marissa file into the office and sit down.

"Dr. Waller, I just want to thank you so much," says Marissa. "Ed has been so calm and so easy to be with. It's like our relationship has a new lease on life."

"I gotta tell you, Doc. I am a whole lot less angry," confirms Ed. "Every time I feel those feelings, I go back to that 'I don't matter' pattern and I see the whole thing. It is getting easier and easier to process through all of that."

"Still watching your thoughts, I assume."

"Always, especially the small thoughts."

"Good for you. That keeps you in Awareness."

"Right on," says Ed.

Marissa gets a concerned look on her face. "Okay, we did Ed. Now it's my turn. I have a problem that I want to solve."

"What is that," I inquire.

"I am a procrastinator. Can you help me with my time management?"

"Of course, but you are going to find that it has nothing to do with time management."

"Really?" Marissa shows me a look of surprise. "I would have guessed . . . I mean I always thought it had to do with time management."

"Let's find out. What is your favorite thing to procrastinate around?"

"Paying the bills," interjects Ed.

"Oh, my gosh, I am so bad at that. I never seem to pay them on time. I just get busy doing other things."

"Okay, so let's do a little experiment to see what comes up. Can we do that?" I ask.

"Sure. Let's get to the bottom of this for heaven's sake."

"Okay, very simple. Just be the watcher and see what comes up. Ready?"

"Ready."

"Marissa, it's time to pay the bills. What's the first thing that comes up?"

"I have to pay them."

"Okay, slow the process down just a little and take another look. It's time to pay the bills."

"Why, why do I have to pay them?"

"Marissa, we are looking for a phrase that a five-year-old would use. You need to pay the bills."

Marissa looks at me and then suddenly says, "I don't want to."

"Right, that's the resistance. You don't like to be told what to do, do you?"

"No, that's for sure."

"Let's try again. It's time to pay the bills."

"You can't make me," Marissa says with a bit of surprise in her voice. "You can't make me?"

"That sounds like what we are looking for. Now look back in your life to when you were a little girl. Who can make you?"

"It feels like I am being forced. Like my father was forcing me to finish my dinner or help in the yard. I just kept thinking, 'you can't make me.'"

"Yep, that sounds like the reactive phrase we are both looking for."

Marissa looks at me in surprise. "'You can't make me?' That's why I don't pay the bills on time?"

"That's exactly right. The voice in your head says, 'you can't make me,' and you don't pay the bills."

"But that doesn't make any sense. I want to pay the bills!"

"Yes, but the monkey thinks your father is telling you to do it. So you get angry and resist being told what to do."

"But I want to pay the bills," Marissa emphasizes.

"It doesn't make sense. As soon as the experience of needing to pay them gets swept into the association of being told to do something by your father, boom, immediate resistance.

"Listen, Marissa, this is not unusual in my experience. I have people in my practice who make up a to-do list and then passively resist it and get nothing done all day long."

"Oh Lord! You are telling me that I am not paying the bills because I am angrily resisting my father? What has the world come to?"

"Precisely. As long as we are asleep and are letting the monkey dictate our behavior, the world will continue to be a very dangerous place."

I give Marissa a few minutes to digest the conversation. Finally, when it seems she is ready for more, I speak up. "Look at Ed, Marissa. Your limbic system thinks that Ed is your father. You have been angrily resisting him in a variety of circumstances almost your entire married life."

"I have? Have I, Ed?"

"It's interesting, but now that I am listening to what he is saying, I realize he is right. I always thought you just really didn't care about me, or that I am the bad one somehow."

"Wow, what is going on here?"

I step in and reassure them both. "Now that you have both made the breakthrough that comes from Witness Thought Transformation™, you will need to watch for this and the other patterns we have talked about."

Marissa says, "Obviously we are not done coming to see you. I had no idea I was doing that. I am sorry Ed, I had no idea."

"Marissa, you need to understand that you are just as angry as Ed. Your anger is just underground. You resist, you withhold, and you cut off the emotional connection between you and Ed. That is how you express your anger. And that's how you punish him. It's called 'passive aggressive behavior.' This is a huge opportunity for you to begin living consciously by being vigilant for this pattern. "

#

Monica slinks into the room. She has a sheepish grin on her face.

"So how is it going?"

"I don't know."

"What do you mean, you don't know?"

"I just don't know. It's weird."

"You mean you had some kind of weird experience, or it's weird coming in here? Or perhaps I am weird."

She chuckles nervously. I wonder what is going on. She has been a bit resistant to learning how to watch her thoughts, but we have a great relationship. At least that's what I thought.

"Okay. I'm going to tell you what happened."

"Fine," I say, "go ahead."

"I have a horrible fear of the dentist. And I had to go to the dentist the other day. I mean I have a horrible fear. I am terrified to go to the dentist."

"Hmmm, okay."

"Well, I was lying there literally shaking. It was the worst experience of my life. I thought I was going to die. I do this every time I go."

I am wondering where this will lead.

"Anyway, I was lying there and I suddenly remembered the thought watching you have been trying to get me to do."

My immediate impression is that she picked the wrong kind of thought to practice Witness Thought Transformation™ on, but I am still interested in where this goes.

"Anyway, the first thing I noticed when I started to become aware of the thoughts was that they were awful thoughts. They were thought like, 'I'm going to die.' 'The Dentist wants to kill me.' They were just horrible thoughts."

No wonder she was shaking and having a panic attack.

"Then the weirdest thing happened."

"What?"

"All the panic went away. I stopped shaking. I just laid there in total peace. The Dentist came in and drilled away, and I couldn't have cared less. It was weird."

My reaction is joy. She has experienced an awakening.

"Welcome to the real world. It must be nice to have that off your back. No more dental fear. But more importantly, you discovered what happens when you awaken. When we believe our thoughts, we endure suffering."

"I don't know it was weird."

"I am not sure I understand. Sounds like you have a breakthrough experience."

"Yeah, I know, but it was weird."

"Weird. You mean the experience freaked you out?"

"Yeah, it was just too weird. Anyway, I have to go back to school next week so I will call you when I want another appointment." With that she hurriedly leaves the room.

I watch her go knowing I may never see her again. She had a breakthrough, she had an "aha" experience, but it was evidently too much for her to handle. I wish she had just practiced on the small thoughts. Truth will break through any opening it can. For her it was too much Truth to handle. The sudden disappearance of drama left her nowhere, which in Truth is where she had always been!

CHAPTER 14: REACTIVE PATTERNS I HAVE KNOWN

When the reactive pattern is finally revealed in the light of the reactive phrase, the holographic image of the entire pattern is revealed for what it is. Just yesterday I had a woman in my office who clearly saw that her jealousy was directly linked to the favoritism shown her brother. At the moment of revelation she was visibly stunned. It is one thing to talk about all of this, but it is quite another to see it rising up inside of you juxtaposed against the backdrop the present moment. There is such a mismatch that it leaves the person absolutely shocked, bemused, and a little disoriented. Often times this reliving brings with it the original pain that accompanies the pattern. More often there is a sense of the total absurdity of it. It is clearly seen as a trick of the mind.

The road to mastery becomes one of constant vigilance. Every reaction becomes an opportunity to stay awake, to see what just happened inside, and to connect the dots to the origin of the pain. This can be as simple as asking oneself "what does this have to do with mom or dad?" With the insight born from Witness Thought Transformation™ the link is instantly revealed and the pattern loses a little more of its power and pain.

Processing the pattern over and over reveals it to be a hijacking generated from our own personal issues that have nothing to do with current reality. The result may not totally extinguish the pattern, but it makes early detection and detachment easier and easier. Over time, detachment takes on the characteristic of a rock in the shoe. A rock is easily dealt with. You merely take off your shoe and throw away the rock. While you may have to deal with the nuisance of another rock someday, discarding it will not be the stuff of drama.

Mastery involves a commitment to capture this limbic hijacker and a resolve to be on guard for the next invasion. With practice and commitment, this all becomes second nature. The one thing we *do* learn from all of this is that our reactions never inform us about the other person; rather the pattern is the book on ourselves, the owner's manual so to speak.

What follows are four of the most common patterns I see every day in my work with people. Remember that even though I have laid these out sequentially, reactive patterns operate in parallel and are holographic, so the parts can never be separated from the whole as far as brain process is concerned.

ANGER

Perhaps there is no more pervasive, talked about pattern than anger. Everyone wants to be less angry or they want someone else to be less angry. You can see below that there are two patterns of anger. The first I have labeled "active anger." This is the kind of anger we think of when we use the word anger; attacking, yelling, defending, screaming, breaking furniture are all behaviors we associate with anger. If we think in terms of fight or flight reactions, active anger belongs in the *fight* category, we might associate anger with that which is predatory rather than prey.

No less important, and certainly no less frequent, is passive anger. Passive anger is the same thing as *passive aggressive behavior*. The key component of this is resistance. You might think of this as noncompliance or lack of cooperation. It is a way of saying "screw you" without using words or a display of anger. Ironically, passive resistance is involved with most procrastination. In my experience, it is the emotional energy behind many extramarital affairs, surprisingly enough. Think of passive resistance as resentment in action, or inaction, as it were.

ACTIVE ANGER

Active anger is driven by a reactive phrase like "doesn't care," "not important," "not good enough," "unwanted," "unloved," and the like. This is reflective of negation or shame, which we will get to in a moment. The perception almost without exception is some kind of rejection or being rejected. Because I am not special, good enough, loved, I am not experiencing the acceptance or approval that I desire.

The principle here is that shame drives anger. Rejection produces feelings of shame. Shame is a sense of being less than, put down, or criticized. Shame is a personal assault on one's worth. Therefore it drives anger. Of course, as children we don't really know how to fight back, but we soon learn.

When we are adults, we interpret various interactions as being shaming, and we fight back with anger. The goal, of course is paradoxical. We want approval, but approval in what form? We want the emotional connection with the *other*. Connection connotes approval. Isn't it ironic that we use anger to get that connection? The fact that this makes no sense seems to be lost on the actively angry. Who, after all, wants to connect with someone who is angry?

Active anger is a genetic predisposition and then is reinforced by a rejecting or shaming parent.

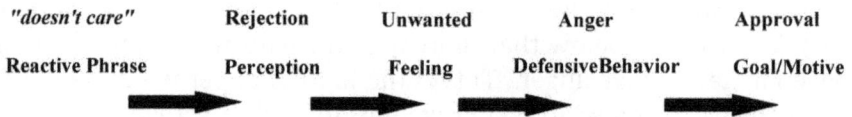

"doesn't care"	Rejection	Unwanted	Anger	Approval
Reactive Phrase	Perception	Feeling	DefensiveBehavior	Goal/Motive
→	→	→	→	

Figure 13: Reactive Pattern for Anger

PASSIVE RESISTANCE

Passive resistance, or passive aggressive behavior, is another form of anger. In contrast with active anger, passive resistance is covert, slick, and often not apparent. Let's say your wife asks you to take out the trash. The passively resistant tactic would be to "forget" to take the trash out. Procrastination is passive anger in action. Basically, passive resistance takes the form of noncooperation or obstruction.

Let's make no mistake about it: passive resistance is violent and hostile and just as abusive as overt anger. Ironically it is a way of acting out anger while looking entirely reasonable at the same time.

Passive resistance is a genetic predisposition just like active anger. Since we are all animals we must have the survival strategies of both predators and prey. But some of us prefer prey strategies over that of the predator. As I discuss extensively in my book, *The Dance of the Lion* sand the Unicorn, this preference is biological. But it does not mean that we are not all capable of passive resistance.

In this type of situation the person has the perception that they are being *controlled* or *pressured*. The reactive phrase can be "you can't make me," or I don't want to," or maybe even simply "no."

Being pressured or controlled makes us angry in this situation and we express the anger through resistance, noncooperation, or obstruction. The goal is to regain our freedom and independence. The insanity of this tactic is that it simply brings on more feelings of being controlled and pressured. If I refuse to take out the garbage it is more than likely that my wife will ask again and again and again!

What is absolutely hilarious about this pattern is that I have had many people in my office who make "to-do" lists for themselves each day. Then they go through their day *resisting* what is on the list because it feels like that parent telling them what to do. The voice in their head is saying "you can't make me," and they resist the to-do list and nothing gets done. Such is the power of the Limbic System. My experience is that all procrastination is a pattern of passive resistance.

For those who prefer covert anger, refusing to have sex or engaging in marital infidelity is almost always passive anger in action. Boy do we miss this one! Even trained professionals can get tricked into thinking that what is actually an act of violence is some other kind of dysfunction. In my office I have counseled a string of passive men who have had affairs strictly as a way of saying, "Screw you. You can't control me." Passive resistance is nothing less than punishment and payback for pressure and control.

Of course, this comes from the unfortunate interaction one has with a controlling and pressuring parent. Often this interaction is viewed as restrictive, bossy, and autocratic; the reaction is extreme anger, usually couched in a persona that comes across as nice, civilized, and overly cooperative. Slick!

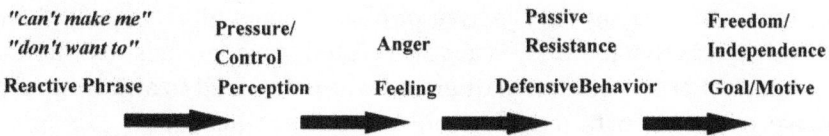

"can't make me" "don't want to"	Pressure/ Control	Anger	Passive Resistance	Freedom/ Independence
Reactive Phrase	Perception	Feeling	DefensiveBehavior	Goal/Motive

Figure 14: Reactive Pattern for Passive Resistance

AVOIDANCE

As I mentioned, we have a preference for predatory or prey strategies. Prey strategies are passive strategies. Avoidance is a form of escape and escape is a very effective strategy to get out of trouble. Those of us who are avoidant hate conflict. It feels unsafe and is very threatening.

The reactive phrase is often something to do with being "in trouble." Sometimes it is "Oh No" or simply "Uh oh." Once this phrase fires off internally, anxiety floods the system. The temptation to flee is overwhelming. This escape takes two forms; emotionally shutting down or literally leaving the scene. Ironically, this tactic nearly always spurs pursuit on the part of the opposite party; they must try even harder to make the connection that is desired.

This avoidance may couple an emotional shutting down with a parasympathetic response to a threat. Paradoxically, while the person may appear to be experiencing no emotions whatsoever, he or she is quaking on the inside.

The goal here is safety. Close personal relationships are threatening and overwhelming, even as they are desired. A person with this pattern is caught between the need for closeness and the need to have distance for safety.

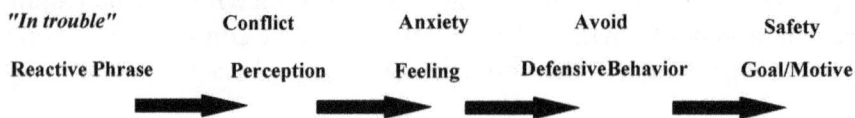

"In trouble"	Conflict	Anxiety	Avoid	Safety
Reactive Phrase	Perception	Feeling	DefensiveBehavior	Goal/Motive

Figure 15: Reactive Pattern for Avoidance

JEALOUSY

I have to admit that jealousy had me stumped for a long time, that is, until I started looking for reactive phrases that might trigger it. What I discovered was that jealousy is always related to a comparison or a rivalry. This means that the person in question was compared to and treated as if they were less important or desirable than the rival.

Normally this is a sibling, although I do believe that sometimes a child can get triangled in between parents, which can create the pattern surrounding jealousy. The reactive phrase is invariably something similar to "they like so-and-so better." So the perception is a comparison, that the child is pitted against some rival for the parent's attention.

Another possible genesis of the jealousy pattern is marital infidelity. Often a parent will involve a child in the drama and constantly program them that the other parent can't be trusted.

The damage that produces jealousy comes developmentally earlier than that of avoidance and anger. The most visible behavior in adults with this pattern is the accusation of betrayal that always accompanies a relentless investigation to find proof. In my office people dig through cell phones, computers, and garages in this search for proof of betrayal.

The fundamental goal or motive for this pattern is to establish *exclusivity* in the relationship. This is a parallel to an attachment crisis that must have happened early in life.

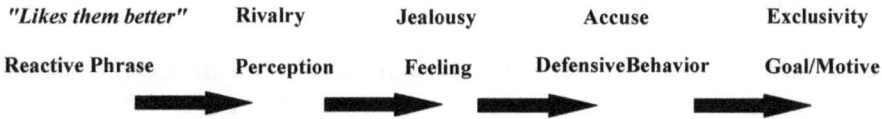

"Likes them better"	Rivalry	Jealousy	Accuse	Exclusivity
Reactive Phrase	Perception	Feeling	DefensiveBehavior	Goal/Motive
➡	➡	➡	➡	

Figure 16: Reactive pattern for jealousy

I am sure there are more reactive phrases and patterns than I have highlighted here. Below is a table of those I have uncovered. I am sure that more will be revealed as time goes on, but I don't suspect there are a great number of them.

Common reactive phrases

Reactive Phrase	Emotion	Behavior	Motive/Goal
in trouble	fear	avoid/escape	safety
uh-oh!	fear	avoid/escape	safety
not good enough	shame	anger	approval
wrong - stupid	shame	anger	approval
nobody cares	shame	anger	approval
watch out	fear	avoid/escape	safety

likes them better	jealousy	accuse	exclusivity
alone	fear	pursue	safety
can't make me	anger	passive resistance	freedom/ independence
don't want to	anger	passive resistance	freedom/ independence
no!	anger	passive resistance	freedom/ independence

FINAL THOUGHTS ON MASTERY

My goal in this chapter was not to make everyone an expert on the patterns. My intent was to provide a road map for those who want to achieve Mastery over their patterns. Once you have identified one of these patterns in yourself, you can easily use *witness consciousness* to track it down through the practice of Witness Thought Transformation™.

The best of all possible places to achieve Mastery is in a relationship since the Limbic System will inevitably take over the relationship and identify the partner as *the parent*. So it really becomes an effort to see what reaction keeps coming up. By using these road maps you will be able to shed more and more light as to what is really happening inside of you.

Essentially every reaction we have is an opportunity to go inside and say "What just happened? How is it related to mom or dad? What is my perception? What feelings am I feeling?" We are keeping ourselves awake when we do this work.

The short cut is to look for the reactive phrase being fired off inside our heads. It is possible, using that method, to catch the pattern whole as it unfolds and tries to hijack the cortex. That *seeing* is a day of liberation. Once the hijacker is seen for what it is and where it came from, it *never again has the same power*. Repetition of the practice makes one more vigilant, quicker to detect the invader, and faster at regaining the equilibrium that Awareness can bring.

CHAPTER 15: DUNCAN AND ED AND MARISSA FINITO

"Look, Duncan, I don't see any real reason for you to come back for more 'therapy.'" I make quotes in the air.

"I know, I know, it's just that I am still a little unsure of myself. I do not want to go back into old patterns under any circumstances."

"I understand, but I will suggest something. Joining a community of people who are awake and watching their thoughts will help you stay in the energy of what you have learned,."

"How do I find them?"

"Well, I have your email and you will be getting announcements. You can also go to my website and see what's going on there. I do have regular teleclasses with people literally from all over the world who are practicing Witness Thought Transformation™. So there are a lot of opportunities to stay in touch."

"Oh, I think I am already getting your emails. I will have to pay a little more attention."

"The important thing is to never stop watching the small thoughts, thoughts about the toothpaste, thoughts about getting your tires rotated. That keeps you in Awareness."

"Then when you start to have a reaction, realize that it is a hijacking and go back to the principles of Mastery that I taught you. Notice everything there is about the hijacker and ask yourself what this has to do with your childhood. Most importantly, try to notice the reactive phrase that starts it all."

"Got it. It seems so simple now, but . . ."

"Right. Now remember, you have a passive system so be especially alert to your avoidance, your shutting down, and how you use passivity to punish your wife."

"I have already discussed it with her. I have told her what to look for and to call it to my attention since I might not always be picking up on it."

"Great, I love when a couple works as a team."

#

Ed and Marisa file into my office and take their usual places.

"We just want to thank you," Ed says. "I guess Pat and Angie were right. They told us this experience would change our entire lives, not just our marriage."

Marissa interjects, "That goes double for me. At the end of the day I can see clearly how this is individual work. But doing the work with a relationship as a backdrop really puts jets on the whole process."

I laugh, "It does if there is no resistance. Too often a couple will come in in arrogance, with a need to be right and self-justified. Then blame takes center stage, and nothing is accomplished. I am honored that you overcame that temptation. This has been nearly effortless for me. For that I thank you."

Ed pipes up, "No, the honor is ours. You have set us free."

"Yes, it is nothing short of a rebirth. In fact this is *the rebirth*," I state. "Where do you go from here?"

"We're not going anywhere," says Marissa. "We are sticking around to help you get your work out to more people. We thought we would get together and talk to Pat and Angie about what we might be able to do to help more people with these principles. Would you make yourself available?"

"Of course I will. By now you realize this practice that I teach has very little to do with therapy, and there is no reason why we shouldn't get it out there in the mainstream. So I appreciate the help."

Marissa tilts her head and says, "You know, since my Awakening, I have been reading books by other Awakened teachers. It all makes sense to me now. I am even reading the Bible through new eyes. The letters of Paul, for instance, talk about what we have been talking about. Right?"

"Yes. Marissa, it looks as if you have launched yourself on a magical journey. I am sure you are going to discover all kinds of wonderful things about your life that you never saw before. I think you will really enjoy reading all of those books and finally understanding exactly what the writer is talking about, because it is now part of your experience."

Conclusion

For years humankind has been in bondage. But we have never known quite how to define that bondage or where it came from. We have known that the *mind* has a lot do to with it. Sages have told us that the mind is like the wind, it's a problem and so on.

The irony is that there is no such thing as a mind. The mind is simply the personification of our own mental activity. Without thought identification, the mind goes away and everything we call *mind* becomes an object in consciousness - in Awareness. We know that this thing called "me," " mine," " myself" is an artifact of the left hemisphere, and the Limbic System and the interplay between vocalization and verbalization. Somehow in the midst of all this we forgot the rest of who we are and we became trapped in our heads.

We live in a world of internal verbal abstraction, carrying on a conversation with no one, but remaining enamored with it. We are so inured that Life itself cannot get our attention.

But along comes a simple little concept, an idea, a definition. Oh, a thought! It is the voice in your head that sounds like you talking to you. It is not the *voice* looking for a *thought*. The voice itself *is* the thought we have been looking for. We have looked for the silence of mind that would reveal our true Self, when all we had to do was to pay attention to the masquerader, the voice that wants to be us. Like Pinocchio who wants to be a real boy, the voice in your head wants to be the real *you*.

Interestingly the entire system of thought depends on us *never looking*. No one has ever bothered to simply look at the speaker. When we do this, the speaker vanishes and instead we are left with the Real, the false having scurried away like a cockroach running from the light.

I have trained hundreds of people in the practice of Witness Thought

Transformation™. Without exception, those who actually do the practice wake up from this mind game. But it is not just a mental transformation; it leads to a spiritual transformation as well. Why would this be? Because the false belief that we are that internal voice keeps us spiritually dead.

Following the simple steps outlined in this book will set you free. It's easy, it's fun, and it takes no effort. Therein lies the problem; the ego mind is not interested in anything easy and fun. However, once convinced, the practitioner finds this simple, elegant little practice to be liberating and life-changing.

But then the need for Mastery appears. We are free, but the temptation to walk back into the fire is strong. We have ego patterns that keep tripping us up. Who would have thought that the glue that holds together these psychological processes was that little voice? I have seen so many of my clients and workshop participants completely blown away when they see these reactive patterns for what they are. The reaction to the revelation is truly amazing, and the aftermath is personal liberation.

The second half of this book outlines a road map for true liberation from these patterns. Look for the voice in your head that goes with your emotional reactions. By turning inward and studying the mind, we can be free.

A Sage of old once described using a thorn to dig out another thorn. Once free, both thorns are thrown away. Using the mind to study the mind is like those two thorns. The freedom of Awareness is experienced as being beyond or outside of the mind. This is the habitat of Awareness. The true Self is that Awareness.

The *me* that we think we are is nothing but a mind pattern. Eventually it can be seen for what it is – just a thought. This limbic/left hemispheric game that we play in our heads keeps us from Truth and Life and the Real. The ego mind thinks it is of great importance. It exalts itself over all. It will not be bowed or humbled.

Awakening and Mastery trump the ego mind, if you are willing to work at it. The loquacious simianus has been caged. While you set yourself free, that monkey may protest, but you are not concerned because finally you can see a vista unlike any other. Life is a brave journey. It is a struggle for freedom and then *living* in the Light.

GLOSSARY

Adult brain: My term for the prefrontal lobes

Amygdala: Two almond shape nuclei buried deep within the Temporal Lobes that are part of the Limbic System and deeply involved in flight or fight, anger, fear and all emotions.

Approach/withdrawal: The asymmetrical response between people of either approaching or withdrawing from stimuli when the central nervous system is aroused.

Attractor pattern: Also called a *Strange Attractor* refers to the tendency of nonlinear data to organize itself into stable patterns. These are described as fractals. This concept is central to Chaos Theory.

Awakening: An aha shift in awareness that feels like being outside oneself. Similar in concept to what some call *Enlightenment*.

Brain lesions: Areas of injury in the brain.

Cerebral Cortex: An extensive sheet of neural tissue that is outermost layer of the brain responsible for higher brain functions.

Chaos Theory: Systems that the theory describes are disordered or nonlinear, yet have an underlying order.

Rene'Descartes: Was a French philosopher, mathematician, physicist, and writer.

Dialogical self: An academic term that means the voice in your head that sound like you talking to you.

Dispositional representations: A term coined by Antonio Damasio that refers to the brains tendency to look for associations.

Ego Mind: Loosely it is the false self, that talks about itself, is only concerned about itself, and whose voice tends to drown out everything else in the mind.

Ego Patterns: Well-defined defensive patterns of perceiving, feeling and reacting based on the programming of early childhood.

Egocentric speech: A type of speech displayed by children that is out loud spoken to oneself, about oneself — a commentary.

Holistic: Looking at the whole or entire rather than looking at parts in isolation from the whole.

Hologram: A 3-dimension image that appears in space when a beam of coherent light is shined through a holographic photographic plate.

Homunculus: Literally means "little man." Refers to the concept that there is a "me" in the head that is at the controls.

Inner speech: The voice in your head that sounds like you talking to you.

Interference pattern: The pattern produced when a beam of coherent light collides with reflected light from an image.

Limbic System: A set of brain structures including the hippocampus, amygdala, anterior thalamic nuclei, and limbic cortex, which support a variety of functions including emotion, behavior, long term memory, and olfaction.

Lion: One of the two types of people from Mark Waller's Lion/Unicorn theory of relationships. The Lion plays the role of the aggressor or pursuer in the relationships and uses predatory strategies.

Mammalian Brain: The Limbic System. The **triune brain** is a model of the evolution of the vertebrate forebrain and behavior proposed by the American physician and neuroscientist Paul D. MacLean. The triune brain consists of the reptilian complex, the paleomammalian complex (limbic system), and the neomammalian complex (neocortex), viewed as structures sequentially added to the forebrain in the course of evolution.

Monkey Brain: Limbic System

Neocortex: Cerebral Cortex

Nonlinear dynamics: Chaos Theory

Passive aggressive: The act of expressing anger, rage, and hostility through obstuction, procrastination, *forgetting*, and noncooperation.

Prefrontal cortex: The prefrontal cortex (PFC) is the anterior part of the frontal lobes of the brain, lying in front of the motor and premotor areas.

Prefrontal lobes: See Prefrontal Cortex

Psychodynamics: A psychological term meaning the effect of childhood development and conditions on adult behavior.

Qualia: A term used in philosophy to describe the subjective quality of conscious experience

Reactive patterns: See ego pattern.

Reactive phrases: A short, declarative predicate that illuminates and activates a reactive pattern or ego pattern.

Recursive: **Recursion** is a method of defining functions in which the function being defined is applied within its own definition. Repeatedly applying function to itself, involving the repeated application of a function to its own values.

Reflexive: Directed back on itself

Repetition compulsion: A psychological phenomenon in which a person repeats a traumatic event or its circumstances over and over again.

Reptilian brain: See Mamillian brain

Right orbital frontal cortex: An area in the right forehead, above the eye socket.

Ritualistic reenactment: Unconsciously repeating patters or behaviors from the past.

Self-reflection: Act of examining one's own internal processes.

Subjectivity: A state of being that cannot be defined in reference to anything else.

Synchronicity: The experience of two or more events that are apparently causally unrelated occurring together in a meaningful manner.

Theta waves: Theta brainwaves are considered extremely relaxing brainwave activity that is commonly associated with sleep and dreaming. Theta brainwaves are high in amplitude and cycle within the range of 4 – 8 Hz.

Thought identified: A phrase that identifies someone who has mistaken themselves to be the voice in their head that sounds like them talking to them.

Trance: An altered state of consciousness.

T.M.: Transcendental meditation is a form of mantra meditation introduced in India in 1955 by Maharishi Mahesh Yogi (1917–2008). Taught in a standardized, seven-step course over 4 days by certified teachers in the United States, it involves the use of a sound or mantra and is practiced for 15–20 minutes twice per day, while sitting comfortably with closed eyes.

Unicorn: One of the two types of people from Mark Waller's Lion/Unicorn theory of relationships. The Unicorn plays the role of the pursuee and uses Prey strategies of avoidance and escape.

Index

BIBLIOGRAPHY

Abraham, D. J. (2004). *The Quest for the Spiritual Neuron.* Koramangala: National Printing Press.

Austin, J. (2000). *Zen and the Brain.* Cambridge: MIT Press.

Becker, A. Weidman, P. (n.d.). *Child Abuse and Neglect.* Retrieved from http://www.mental-health-matters.com: http://www.mental-health-matters.com/articles/article.php?artID=581.

Bolte Taylor, J. My Stroke of Insight (New York: Viking, 2006)

D'Esposito, C. R. (2005). Directing the mind's eye: prefrontal, inferior and medial temporal mechanisms for visual working memory. *Current Opinion in Neurobiology, 15,* 175–182.

Damasio, A. (1994). *Descartes' Error.* New York: G.P. Putnam's Sons.

Damasio, A. (1999). *The Feeling of What Happens.* New York: Harcourt Brace and Company.

Damasio, A. (2003). *Looking for Spinoza.* New York: Harcourt, Inc.

Davidson, H. H. (2004). Disambiguating the Components of Emotional Regulation. *Child Development, 75* (2), 361-365.

Davidson, R. (2004). The privileged status of emotion in the brain. *The Proceedings of the National Accademy of Sciences, 101* (33), 11915–11916.

Davidson, R. J. (2004). What does the prefrontal cortex "do" in affect: Perspectives on frontal EEG asymmetry research. *Biological Psychology, 67,* 219–233.

D'Esposito, B. R. (1999). The roles of prefrontal brain regions in components of working memory: Effects of memory load and individual differences. *Proceedings of the National Academy of Sciences, 96* (11), 6558-6563.

Freeman, W. J. (n.d.). *Emotion is Essential to All Intentional Behaviors.* Retrieved from http://sulcus.berkeley.edu: http://sulcus.berkeley.edu/ wjf/CE. Neurodynamics.and.Emotion.pdf.

Freeman, W. J. (n.d.). *Walter J. Freeman.* Retrieved from Walter J. Freeman: http://sulcus.berkeley.edu.

Freeman, W. J. (2000). Perception of time and causation through the kinesthesia of intentional action. *Cognitive Processing, 1.*

Freeman, W. J. (2001). Bridging the Gaps Between Neuron, Brain and Behavior with Neurodynamics. *Jean Piaget Society Symposium.* Berkeley.

Freeman, W. J. (2001). *How Brains Make Up Their Minds.* New York: Columbia University Press.

Freeman, W. J. (2004). *Mass Action in the Nervous System.* New York: Academic Press.

Hawkins, D. (2001). *The Eye of the I.* W. Sedona: Veritas.

Hawkins, D. (2003). *Reality and Subjectivity.* W. Sedona: Veritas.

Hermans, H. J. (2002). The Dialogical Self as a Society of Mind: Introduction. *Theory & Psychology, 12* (2), 147-160.

Hiroshi Yamasaki, K. S. (2002). Dissociable prefrontal brain systems for attention and emotion. *Proceedings of the National Accademy of Sciences, 99* (17), 11447-11451.

Irwin, W. (2004). Amygdalar interhemispheric functional connectivity differs between the non-depressed and depressed human brain. *NeuroImage, 21,* 674– 686.

Jaynes, J. (1976). *The Origin of Consciousness in the Breakdown of the Bicameral Mind.* Boston: Houghton Mifflin.

Johnston, V. (1999). *Why We Feel: The Science of Human Emotions.* Cambridge: Helix.

Kline, J. (1998). Is Left Frontal Brain Activation in Defensiveness Gender Specific? *Journal of Abnormal Psychology, 107* (1), 149-153.

Lewis, M. D. (2002). The Dialogical Brain: Contributions of Emotional Neurobiology to Understanding the Dialogical Self. *Theory & Psychology, 12* (2), 175-190.

Martensson, L. (1997, September 16th). Love, Hope & Brain Science. *Based on a public lecture at the University of Oslo*. Oslo, Norway.

Matute, H. (n.d.). *Inferring Causality and Making Predictions. Some Misconceptions in the Animal and Human Learning Literature*. Retrieved from www.interdisciplines.org: http://www.interdisciplines.org/causality/papers/16.

Ouspensky, P. (1949). *In Search of the Miraculous*. New York: Hartcourt Brace & Company.

Ouspensky, P. (1971). *The Fourth Way*. New York: Vintage.

Pinker, S. (1997). *How the Mind Works*. New York: W. W. Norton.

Rogers, L. (2001). *Sexing the Brain*. New York: Columbia University Press.

Shallice, T. (2001). Theory of mind and the prefrontal cortex. *Brain, 124* (2), 247-248.

Siegel, D. (1999). *The Developing Mind*. New York: the Guilford Press.

Tolle, E. (1999). *The Power of Now*. Novatno: New World Library.

Tononi, E. &. (2000). *A Universe of Consciousness*. New York: Basic Books.

Valsiner, J. (2002). Forms of Dialogical Relations and Semiotic Autoregulation within the Self. *Theory & Psychology, 12* (2), 251-265.

Vygotsky, L. (1986). *Thought and Language*. Cambridge: the MIT Press.

Watzlawick, P. (1974). *Change*. New York: W. W. Norton.

Williams LM, L. B. (n.d.). Amygdala-prefrontal dissociation of subliminal and supraliminal fear. *Human Brain Mapping. 2006; 27:652-661*

ABOUT MARK WALLER

Mark Waller is the award winning author of four books and numerous articles. A licensed Marriage and Family Therapist, he has been a management consultant for over ten years and has conducted workshops for manufacturers, utilities, and the computer industry. He has lectured at the University of Wisconsin and George Washington University. Mark has a BA in Business, a Masters Degree in Marital and Family Therapy, and a Ph.D. in Psychology.

At 40, he was a successful technical consultant, and the author of three books on computers and electrical power. His first book was entitled *Computer Electrical Power Requirements*. His second book, *PC Power Protection*, was a Tab Book Club main selection. His third book, *Mark Waller's Harmonics*, established him as an acknowledged leader in the field of electrical power quality. He received The Award of Achievement from the Society of Technical Communications in the 1988-89 Competition for an article written for *Byte Magazine*. At that time, he was named a "Finalist" in L. Ron Hubbard's "Writers of the Future" contest (he is not a Scientologist). He traveled the country giving workshops and consulting for companies such as Southern California Edison and The Jet Propulsion Laboratory. He taught classes at Georgetown University and the University of Wisconsin.

Then disaster struck. Mark had a midlife crisis and became a statistic. The economy, the marriage, and the lifestyle all collapsed at the same time. Mark had nothing left but pain and fear. During this dark night of the soul Mark experienced an ***awakening***. This led to a career and life change. His books, *The Dance of the Lion and the Unicorn* and *Awakening* were born during new insight that followed.

Today Mark is a Licensed Marriage and Family Therapist in Central California where he lives with his wife Sheila. His passion is helping others experience an *Awakening* as well.

OTHER BOOKS BY MARK WALLER

Awakening: Exposing the Voice of the Mosaic Mind

The Dance of the Lion and the Unicorn: the Secret of Conscious Relationships

Beyond the Paradox of Being Human

For a complete listing of books and other learning material, please go to:
www.masteringthought.com

www.ingramcontent.com/pod-product-compliance
Lightning Source LLC
Chambersburg PA
CBHW030020290326

41934CB00005B/413